JUMBLE® Jailbreak

These Puzzles are on the Loose!

**Henri Arnold
and
Bob Lee**

TRIUMPH
B O O K S

This book is available in quantity at special discounts
for your group or organization.

For further information, contact:

Triumph Books LLC
814 North Franklin Street
Chicago, Illinois 60610
Phone: (312) 337-0747
www.triumphbooks.com

Printed in U.S.A.

ISBN: 978-1-62937-002-6

Design by Sue Knopf

CONTENTS

JUMBLE

JAILBREAK

Classic Puzzles

JUMBLE®

Unscramble these four Jumbles, one letter to each square, to form four ordinary words.

LARNS

BOGUM

CROFIL

SCEBIT

WHAT THE NEUROSURGEON'S IDEA WAS.

Now arrange the circled letters to form the surprise answer, as suggested by the above cartoon.

Print answer here **A**

2

JUMBLE®

Unscramble these four Jumbles, one letter to
each square, to form four ordinary words.

MYKUR

INHEW

YECKAL

DELPOW

... all a mistake
... didn't mean ...

WHAT THE SNAKE IN
THE GRASS DID WHEN
HE WAS CAUGHT IN
THE ACT.

Now arrange the circled letters to form
the surprise answer, as suggested by the
above cartoon.

**Print answer
here** ⬡⬡⬡⬡⬡⬡ **HIS** ⬡⬡⬡ **OUT**

JUMBLE®

Unscramble these four Jumbles, one letter to
each square, to form four ordinary words.

DUTEE

RUYLS

CLAMBE

GROAFE

Ugh!

HOW THE PORTRAIT
PAINTER EXPRESSED
HIMSELF.

Now arrange the circled letters to form
the surprise answer, as suggested by the
above cartoon.

Print answer here **HE** ⬡⬡⬡⬡ ⬡⬡⬡⬡⬡

JUMBLE.

Unscramble these four Jumbles, one letter to
each square, to form four ordinary words.

WONIG

TYRID

TRUJIS

GOOSTE

Poker . . . sick friend . . . traffic

HOW THE PRETZEL
MAKER GOT
HIS ALIBI.

Now arrange the circled letters to form
the surprise answer, as suggested by the
above cartoon.

Print answer here

5

JUMBLE®

Unscramble these four Jumbles, one letter to
each square, to form four ordinary words.

Er . . . uh . . .
sweetheart
. . . glub . . .

Huh! The strong
silent type!

YALLD

BOARR

PREJUM

NICKES

WHEN IT COMES
TO WORDS THIS GUY
DOESN'T HAVE MUCH
OF A FLOW.

Now arrange the circled letters to form
the surprise answer, as suggested by the
above cartoon.

Print answer here

JUMBLE®

Unscramble these four Jumbles, one letter to each square, to form four ordinary words.

KEHRI

NYSOW

BEMFUL

FEEDAC

Waist: 56 . . . and ¼ . . .
Seat: 66 . . . and ⅞ . . .
Length: 21 . . . and ⅜ . . .

HOW THE PRECISE TAILOR SPOKE.

Now arrange the circled letters to form the surprise answer, as suggested by the above cartoon.

Print answer here IN ⬭⬭⬭⬭⬭⬭⬭⬭⬭ **TONES**

JUMBLE®

Unscramble these four Jumbles, one letter to
each square, to form four ordinary words.

CYDER

MUJOB

SIFUNE

THAGUT

THIS COULD BE
THE DIFFERENCE
BETWEEN MALE
AND FEMALE.

Now arrange the circled letters to form
the surprise answer, as suggested by the
above cartoon.

Print answer here **AN** ⬡⬡⬡⬡⬡⬡⬡⬡⬡

8

JUMBLE®

Unscramble these four Jumbles, one letter to each square, to form four ordinary words.

YURLT

SHWIK

ONASAT

TEVVLE

WHAT GOLD DIGGERS GO FOR IN ORDER TO GET DIAMONDS.

Now arrange the circled letters to form the surprise answer, as suggested by the above cartoon.

Print answer here

JUMBLE®

Unscramble these four Jumbles, one letter to each square, to form four ordinary words.

ELVOH

TIPAL

TARECE

CLOASE

Fellows . . .
THIS CAN BE
IRRITATING AS WELL
AS FOOLISH.

Now arrange the circled letters to form the surprise answer, as suggested by the above cartoon.

Print answer here

JUMBLE®

Unscramble these four Jumbles, one letter to
each square, to form four ordinary words.

HEMIC

RAHOY

WEKERS

THAGAS

SOME GI'S CONSIDER
THIS THE SLOPPIEST
PART OF THE ARMY.

Now arrange the circled letters to form
the surprise answer, as suggested by the
above cartoon.

Print answer here

11

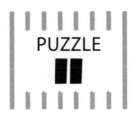
JUMBLE®

Unscramble these four Jumbles, one letter to
each square, to form four ordinary words.

ACHOM

MUPLE

GLAJEN

SCAFIO

Again?

She'll be with
you in a
moment

WHY THEY CALLED
THE DIZZY BLONDE
"BUBBLE HEAD."

Now arrange the circled letters to form
the surprise answer, as suggested by the
above cartoon.

*Print
answer
here*   SHE WAS ALWAYS

JUMBLE®

Unscramble these four Jumbles, one letter to
each square, to form four ordinary words.

GURAU

HICED

TURBLE

CLAUNY

Make
any
money
today?

THIS MIGHT MEAN
NOTHING'S BEEN
TAKEN IN.

Now arrange the circled letters to form
the surprise answer, as suggested by the
above cartoon.

Print answer here

JUMBLE®

Unscramble these four Jumbles, one letter to
each square, to form four ordinary words.

RUSIV

NOPUD

DUCADE

HEBLED

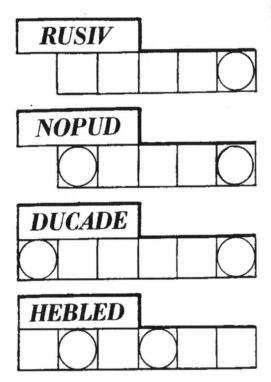

THE KIND OF CREATURES
YOU MIGHT SEE IN
LOW-DOWN DIVES.

Now arrange the circled letters to form
the surprise answer, as suggested by the
above cartoon.

Print answer here

JUMBLE

Unscramble these four Jumbles, one letter to
each square, to form four ordinary words.

THICH

DASIT

CUTLED

INJEYT

THIS GETS LONGER
EVERY TIME
YOU CUT IT.

Now arrange the circled letters to form
the surprise answer, as suggested by the
above cartoon.

Print answer here **A** ◯◯◯◯◯

JUMBLE®

Unscramble these four Jumbles, one letter to
each square, to form four ordinary words.

WORNC

DINEK

PINKAD

INBENG

WHAT YOU MIGHT
EXPECT DONKEYS'
MILK TO HAVE.

Now arrange the circled letters to form
the surprise answer, as suggested by the
above cartoon.

Print answer here A ⬡⬡⬡⬡ ⬡⬡ **IT**

JUMBLE®

Unscramble these four Jumbles, one letter to
each square, to form four ordinary words.

LIWLT

YOBOT

THINGK

STEJAM

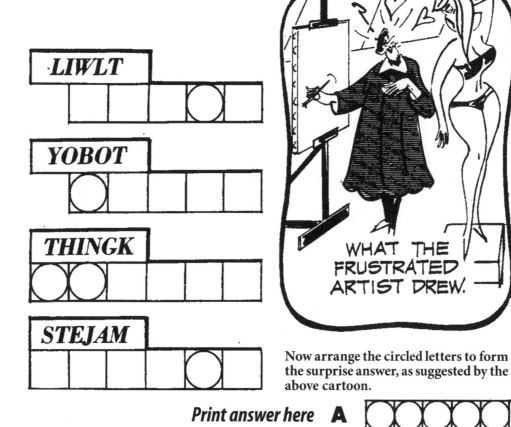

Get lost!

WHAT THE
FRUSTRATED
ARTIST DREW.

Now arrange the circled letters to form
the surprise answer, as suggested by the
above cartoon.

Print answer here **A**

JUMBLE®

Unscramble these four Jumbles, one letter to each square, to form four ordinary words.

VEGIN

HOWSY

WEDDEG

BENEAT

Such a sweeping statement!

THIS OFTEN COVERS A LOT!

Now arrange the circled letters to form the surprise answer, as suggested by the above cartoon.

Print answer here

JUMBLE®

Unscramble these four Jumbles, one letter to each square, to form four ordinary words.

YOWLL

REGUP

ROTTAH

ABBIDE

Two bucks on my kid

A GOOD BET FOR FIRST GRADERS.

Now arrange the circled letters to form the surprise answer, as suggested by the above cartoon.

Print answer here **THE**

JUMBLE®

Unscramble these four Jumbles, one letter to
each square, to form four ordinary words.

ENWIC

TARFD

HACING

BLUTSY

You win, dear

WHY THE SNAKE LOST
THE ARGUMENT.

Now arrange the circled letters to form
the surprise answer, as suggested by the
above cartoon.

Print
answer
here

HE DIDN'T HAVE A ◯◯◯ TO ◯◯◯◯◯◯ ON

JUMBLE.

Unscramble these four Jumbles, one letter to
each square, to form four ordinary words.

RELEC

TARIE

WOBELL

DOVERN

THIS GUY MIGHT TELL
YOU A STORY WITH A
SLANT TO IT.

Now arrange the circled letters to form
the surprise answer, as suggested by the
above cartoon.

*Print
answer
here* **ONE WHO'S** ⬡⬡⬡ **ON THE** ⬡⬡⬡⬡⬡

JUMBLE®

Unscramble these four Jumbles, one letter to
each square, to form four ordinary words.

SNALT

SATHY

CHABER

ROMMAT

WHY THE UNSUCCESSFUL
TENNIS PLAYER
WAS OFFERED A
CIGARETTE LIGHTER.

Now arrange the circled letters to form
the surprise answer, as suggested by the
above cartoon.

*Print
answer
here* **HE** ☐☐☐☐☐ **ALL HIS** ☐☐☐☐☐☐☐

JUMBLE®

Unscramble these four Jumbles, one letter to
each square, to form four ordinary words.

HUTEC

ANUFA

BITSUM

GURDIT

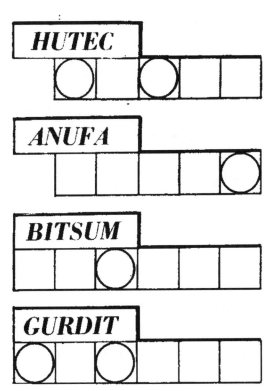

WHERE A PEDESTRIAN
MIGHT FEEL ON EDGE.

Now arrange the circled letters to form
the surprise answer, as suggested by the
above cartoon.

Print answer here **THE**

JUMBLE®

Unscramble these four Jumbles, one letter to
each square, to form four ordinary words.

ETHIL

TILOP

SNAZAT

HARGIS

WHAT YOU MIGHT FIND
IN THAT OL'
SWIMMIN' HOLE.

Now arrange the circled letters to form
the surprise answer, as suggested by the
above cartoon.

Print answer here "◯◯◯◯◯ – ◯◯◯◯◯"

JUMBLE®

Unscramble these four Jumbles, one letter to each square, to form four ordinary words.

LALIV

VYNER

TUNBOY

REVEWS

A KIND OF EMPLOYEE THAT MIGHT BE FOUND IN *TAVERNS.*

Now arrange the circled letters to form the surprise answer, as suggested by the above cartoon.

Print answer here

JUMBLE®

Unscramble these four Jumbles, one letter to
each square, to form four ordinary words.

ASAIL

HORTT

KEBTUC

MEDOCY

WHAT A BOY WHO
HATES BOOKS MIGHT
PREFER TO DO.

Now arrange the circled letters to form
the surprise answer, as suggested by the
above cartoon.

Print answer here

26

JUMBLE®

JAILBREAK

Daily Puzzles

JUMBLE®

Unscramble these four Jumbles, one letter to
each square, to form four ordinary words.

YARDT

HESEP

MOANAZ

TRUIPY

What a
ham!

WHAT THE BUTCHER
TURNED ACTOR GOT.

Now arrange the circled letters to form
the surprise answer, as suggested by the
above cartoon.

Print answer here

JUMBLE®

Unscramble these four Jumbles, one letter to
each square, to form four ordinary words.

ILLAC

PITSE

WOAMED

SABBOR

Sorry, but I'll be busy

WHAT THE HORSE
WHO FLIRTED WITH
THE MARE IN THE
STABLE GOT.

Now arrange the circled letters to form
the surprise answer, as suggested by the
above cartoon.

Print answer here **THE** ⬡⬡⬡⬡ **OLD** ⬡⬡⬡⬡⬡

JUMBLE®

Unscramble these four Jumbles, one letter to
each square, to form four ordinary words.

TURTE

PROUG

NEETIC

STELEN

WHY THEY COULDN'T
FIND THE
FENCING MASTER.

Now arrange the circled letters to form
the surprise answer, as suggested by the
above cartoon.

*Print
answer
here*   **HE WAS**   " ☐☐☐ **TO** ☐☐☐☐☐☐ "

JUMBLE®

Unscramble these four Jumbles, one letter to
each square, to form four ordinary words.

PORRI

WENIT

PEXLUD

MANDOR

WHAT A MAN WHO
COULDN'T HOLD HIS
LIQUOR DID.

Now arrange the circled letters to form
the surprise answer, as suggested by the
above cartoon.

Print answer here

JUMBLE®

Unscramble these four Jumbles, one letter to
each square, to form four ordinary words.

SNAIE

WARLD

CELTIN

MECION

WHAT SKYWRITERS
WRITE.

Which
one,
sir?

ACME   SPEEDY

Now arrange the circled letters to form
the surprise answer, as suggested by the
above cartoon.

Print answer here

JUMBLE®

Unscramble these four Jumbles, one letter to each square, to form four ordinary words.

BLACE

YUNIF

SPEGOL

CHUPIC

They got me!

WHAT THE EXTERMINATOR MADE THE ANTS DO.

Now arrange the circled letters to form the surprise answer, as suggested by the above cartoon.

Print answer here

33

JUMBLE®

Unscramble these four Jumbles, one letter to
each square, to form four ordinary words.

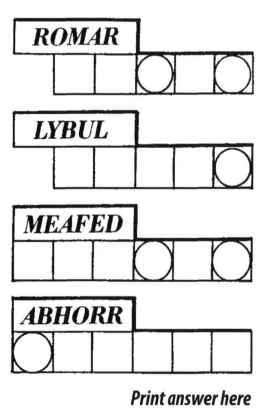

ROMAR

LYBUL

MEAFED

ABHORR

THE ALCOHOLIC ACTOR'S
FAVORITE SANDWICH.

Now arrange the circled letters to form
the surprise answer, as suggested by the
above cartoon.

Print answer here ⬡⬡⬡ **ON** ⬡⬡⬡

JUMBLE®

Unscramble these four Jumbles, one letter to each square, to form four ordinary words.

COUFS

HOCAP

TICHEC

FITANN

HOW THE
CORRESPONDENCE
ROMANCE ENDED.

Now arrange the circled letters to form the surprise answer, as suggested by the above cartoon.

Print answer here   **IN A**

JUMBLE®

Unscramble these four Jumbles, one letter to
each square, to form four ordinary words.

BRILO

VOLEN

CALAPE

BRATIB

WHAT THE BABY WHO
FIRST SAW THE LIGHT OF
DAY ON A PLANE WAS.

Now arrange the circled letters to form
the surprise answer, as suggested by the
above cartoon.

Print answer here " ☐☐☐ – ☐☐☐☐ "

JUMBLE®

Unscramble these four Jumbles, one letter to
each square, to form four ordinary words.

KAROC

SYNAP

NUBONI

GLEENT

We want
our money
back!

WHAT THE NUDE SHOW
TURNED OUT TO BE.

Now arrange the circled letters to form
the surprise answer, as suggested by the
above cartoon.

Print answer here **A** ☐◯◯◯ – ◯◯☐

JUMBLE®

Unscramble these four Jumbles, one letter to
each square, to form four ordinary words.

SUYFS

TOROB

VOUDER

RENITE

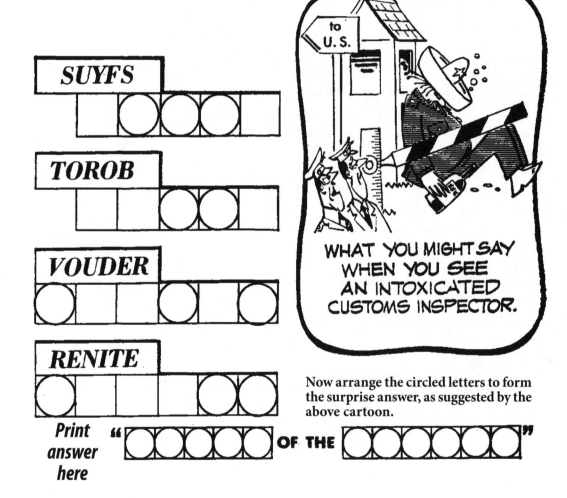

WHAT YOU MIGHT SAY
WHEN YOU SEE
AN INTOXICATED
CUSTOMS INSPECTOR.

Now arrange the circled letters to form
the surprise answer, as suggested by the
above cartoon.

Print
answer
here "⃝⃝⃝⃝⃝ OF THE ⃝⃝⃝⃝⃝⃝⃝"

JUMBLE®

Unscramble these four Jumbles, one letter to
each square, to form four ordinary words.

OSLOE

CLAME

LAFTER

TEECIX

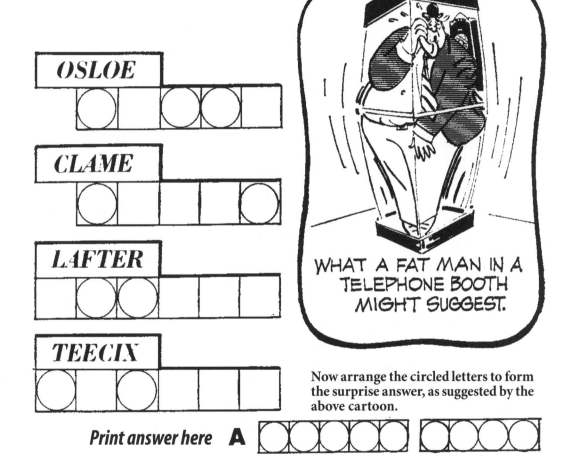

WHAT A FAT MAN IN A
TELEPHONE BOOTH
MIGHT SUGGEST.

Now arrange the circled letters to form
the surprise answer, as suggested by the
above cartoon.

Print answer here **A**

JUMBLE®

Unscramble these four Jumbles, one letter to
each square, to form four ordinary words.

ROMIN

○○ ○○

USHOE

○ ○○

GANOLS

○○○ ○

ATRILA

○ ○

Gosh,
it's
2 A.M.!

WHEN LOVERS
OFTEN HAVE THEIR
BIG MOMENTS.

Now arrange the circled letters to form
the surprise answer, as suggested by the
above cartoon.

*Print answer
here* **IN THE** ○○○○○ ○○○○○

JUMBLE®

Unscramble these four Jumbles, one letter to
each square, to form four ordinary words.

IRFEY

NAPAG

BOILEM

RIMPIA

WHERE YOU
MIGHT GET MAIL
IN OHIO.

Now arrange the circled letters to form
the surprise answer, as suggested by the
above cartoon.

Print answer here **FROM** ☐☐☐☐

JUMBLE®

Unscramble these four Jumbles, one letter to
each square, to form four ordinary words.

VILEA

NUKKS

REMUDE

SEPPOO

My, my!

WHAT A LITTLE SOFT
SOAP CAN MAKE.

Now arrange the circled letters to form
the surprise answer, as suggested by the
above cartoon.

Print answer here **A**

JUMBLE®

Unscramble these four Jumbles, one letter to
each square, to form four ordinary words.

COEMA

OMPET

BANACA

EPITOC

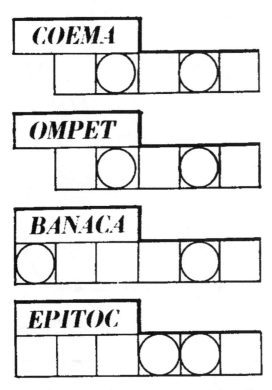

WHAT SOME POLITICIANS
SEEM TO WANT
TO TAX MOST.

Now arrange the circled letters to form
the surprise answer, as suggested by the
above cartoon.

Print answer here **OUR**

JUMBLE®

Unscramble these four Jumbles, one letter to each square, to form four ordinary words.

TEBER

POREA

MANIAE

CHOPON

Happy birthday!

Outrate AIRLINES

THE CHEAPEST WAY TO GET TO EUROPE.

Now arrange the circled letters to form the surprise answer, as suggested by the above cartoon.

Print answer here **BE**

JUMBLE®

Unscramble these four Jumbles, one letter to
each square, to form four ordinary words.

DUCIL

VOACH

RACCIT

POYNAC

Psst! I hear we're all getting raises!

Huh! Just another rumor!

THIS MIGHT BE A BREAK
IF YOU'RE A WORKING
PERSON, BUT YOU CAN'T
BANK ON IT!

Now arrange the circled letters to form
the surprise answer, as suggested by the
above cartoon.

Print answer here **A**

JUMBLE®

Unscramble these four Jumbles, one letter to
each square, to form four ordinary words.

RALVO

GEFUD

BROCAN

RIMMOE

WHEN IT'S WET,
GET UNDER IT!

Now arrange the circled letters to form
the surprise answer, as suggested by the
above cartoon.

Print answer here

JUMBLE®

Unscramble these four Jumbles, one letter to each square, to form four ordinary words.

WAQUS

SMUNI

TEASTE

MADGEA

Not his real name

Nothing ELSE real, either!

WHAT THE BEWIGGED ACTOR PERFORMED UNDER.

Now arrange the circled letters to form the surprise answer, as suggested by the above cartoon.

Print answer here **AN** ☐☐☐☐☐☐☐ ☐☐☐☐

JUMBLE®

Unscramble these four Jumbles, one letter to
each square, to form four ordinary words.

RICOU

KOSTE

THODEB

NATIED

THE DEBTOR'S MOTTO.

Now arrange the circled letters to form
the surprise answer, as suggested by the
above cartoon.

Print answer here " ◯◯◯ **UNTO** ◯◯◯◯◯◯ "

JUMBLE®

Unscramble these four Jumbles, one letter to each square, to form four ordinary words.

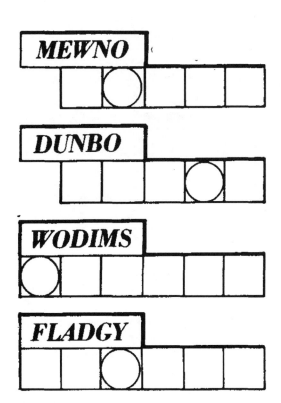

MEWNO

DUNBO

WODIMS

FLADGY

Sick . . . can't get up to go to school . . .

OK

LYING LIKE THIS CAN BE EASY!

Now arrange the circled letters to form the surprise answer, as suggested by the above cartoon.

Print answer here ◯◯◯◯

JUMBLE®

Unscramble these four Jumbles, one letter to
each square, to form four ordinary words.

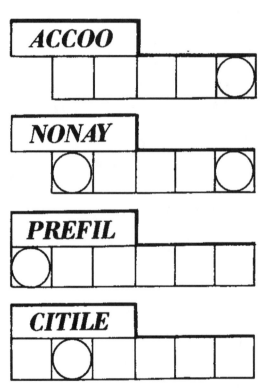

ACCOO

NONAY

PREFIL

CITILE

4TH YEAR

Great
story—
human
interest

IN THE LONG RUN,
THIS WILL BENEFIT
A WRITER!

Now arrange the circled letters to form
the surprise answer, as suggested by the
above cartoon.

Print answer here

50

JUMBLE®

Unscramble these four Jumbles, one letter to each square, to form four ordinary words.

He's such a good boy

WHAT LITTLE LAMBS OFTEN PULL.

YOLID

GEDEW

REBOOL

GORNTS

Now arrange the circled letters to form the surprise answer, as suggested by the above cartoon.

Print answer here THE ⭕⭕⭕⭕ OVER YOUR ⭕⭕⭕⭕

JUMBLE®

Unscramble these four Jumbles, one letter to
each square, to form four ordinary words.

That'll wow him!

SHEER BLOUSES

TO GET A HEAVY
DATE WEAR THIS.

LOGAT

YAHIR

NIPURT

HESTEE

Now arrange the circled letters to form
the surprise answer, as suggested by the
above cartoon.

Print answer here **SOMETHING**

JUMBLE®

Unscramble these four Jumbles, one letter to
each square, to form four ordinary words.

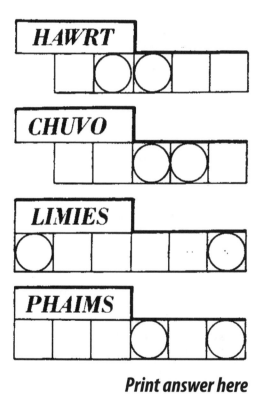

HAWRT

CHUVO

LIMIES

PHAIMS

Am I late, dear?

THE ONLY THING
SOME WOMEN EVER
DO ON TIME.

Now arrange the circled letters to form
the surprise answer, as suggested by the
above cartoon.

Print answer here

JUMBLE®

Unscramble these four Jumbles, one letter to
each square, to form four ordinary words.

OXTIN

REQUE

DRUPAW

GLINJE

A MORE LASTING
FINISH FOR A CAR
THAN LACQUER.

Now arrange the circled letters to form
the surprise answer, as suggested by the
above cartoon.

Print answer here ◯◯◯◯◯◯◯

JUMBLE®

Unscramble these four Jumbles, one letter to
each square, to form four ordinary words.

PLYSH

MARRE

PLUBAR

TYMINE

THE DIFFERENCE
BETWEEN A GOOD SPEECH
AND A BAD ONE.

Now arrange the circled letters to form
the surprise answer, as suggested by the
above cartoon.

Print answer here

JUMBLE®

Unscramble these four Jumbles, one letter to each square, to form four ordinary words.

SENWY

DUGAR

ROTHEX

PERTAT

WHAT A LOT OF MARRIAGE TIES ARE SEVERED BY.

Now arrange the circled letters to form the surprise answer, as suggested by the above cartoon.

Print answer here **A**

JUMBLE®

Unscramble these four Jumbles, one letter to
each square, to form four ordinary words.

CARTT

AFESH

NEEXTT

BLIDIO

WHAT THE LAWYER
SAID AS HE ATE
AN OYSTER.

Now arrange the circled letters to form
the surprise answer, as suggested by the
above cartoon.

**Print answer
here** HMMM —

JUMBLE®

Unscramble these four Jumbles, one letter to each square, to form four ordinary words.

LIEBE

DILEY

BINNOR

TAIGER

THIS MIGHT BE THE LATEST THING IN WEDDINGS!

Now arrange the circled letters to form the surprise answer, as suggested by the above cartoon.

Print answer here **THE** ◯◯◯◯◯

JUMBLE®

Unscramble these four Jumbles, one letter to
each square, to form four ordinary words.

REBLY

GOFOR

YERTAW

HUSTYP

I love
you

GIVES A BEATING
THAT LASTS A
LIFETIME.

Now arrange the circled letters to form
the surprise answer, as suggested by the
above cartoon.

Print answer here

JUMBLE®

Unscramble these four Jumbles, one letter to
each square, to form four ordinary words.

GYTAN

YIHFS

WELBIA

PALLOW

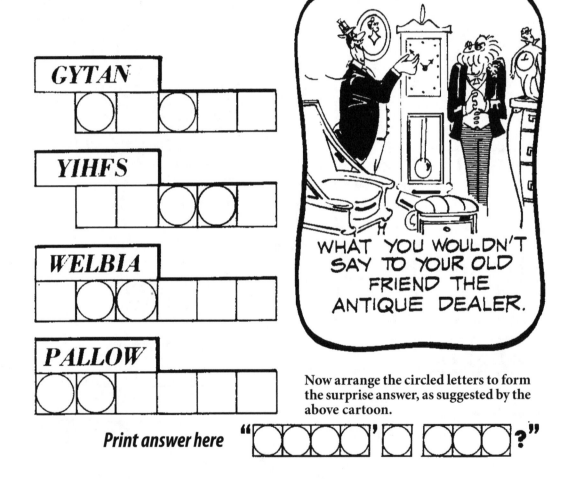

WHAT YOU WOULDN'T
SAY TO YOUR OLD
FRIEND THE
ANTIQUE DEALER.

Now arrange the circled letters to form
the surprise answer, as suggested by the
above cartoon.

Print answer here "◯◯◯◯◯'◯ ◯◯◯?"

JUMBLE®

Unscramble these four Jumbles, one letter to
each square, to form four ordinary words.

KAHIK

DONSY

FITHES

YARQUR

WHAT A MAN WHO
DRINKS LIKE A FISH
RARELY DRINKS.

Now arrange the circled letters to form
the surprise answer, as suggested by the
above cartoon.

**Print answer
here**   WHAT A

JUMBLE®

Unscramble these four Jumbles, one letter to
each square, to form four ordinary words.

NUFTO

CLOAV

SPUMGY

LOONED

WHAT THEY DANCED
DURING THE
PRISON BREAK.

Now arrange the circled letters to form
the surprise answer, as suggested by the
above cartoon.

Print answer here **THE "☐☐☐☐ – ☐☐"**

JUMBLE®

Unscramble these four Jumbles, one letter to each square, to form four ordinary words.

AWNTY

EXVIN

LARMIN

THIGEY

GROWING OLD ISN'T SO BAD IF YOU CONSIDER THIS.

Gone! All gone!

But (chuckle) WE'RE not!

Now arrange the circled letters to form the surprise answer, as suggested by the above cartoon.

Print answer here **THE** ◯◯◯◯◯◯◯◯◯◯◯◯◯◯

JUMBLE®

Unscramble these four Jumbles, one letter to
each square, to form four ordinary words.

MAITY

RECSS

PREDIM

UNSADE

Whew! Just
made it!

More dough
next month

WHAT BOTH LANDLORDS
AND TENANTS OFTEN
TRY TO DO.

Now arrange the circled letters to form
the surprise answer, as suggested by the
above cartoon.

Print answer here ◯◯◯◯◯ **THE** ◯◯◯◯

JUMBLE®

Unscramble these four Jumbles, one letter to
each square, to form four ordinary words.

TIBEF

KARIF

DOALUN

SOUMUC

She was a
knockout

WHAT HAPPENED TO
THE GIRL WITH THE
HOURGLASS FIGURE?

Now arrange the circled letters to form
the surprise answer, as suggested by the
above cartoon.

Print answer here ⬡⬡⬡⬡ ⬡⬡⬡ **OUT**

JUMBLE®

Unscramble these four Jumbles, one letter to
each square, to form four ordinary words.

BOZIM

KRYJE

EBONGY

HYDING

WHAT THOSE WHO DRINK
TO FORGET ALWAYS
SEEM TO REMEMBER.

Now arrange the circled letters to form
the surprise answer, as suggested by the
above cartoon.

Print answer here **TO** ⬡⭘⭘⭘⭘⭘

JUMBLE®

Unscramble these four Jumbles, one letter to
each square, to form four ordinary words.

YAASS

HOTYM

TEAZOL

PINGYT

Poor
little
tot

WHAT A BABY MIGHT
BE IN WARM WEATHER

Now arrange the circled letters to form
the surprise answer, as suggested by the
above cartoon.

Print answer here **A**

JUMBLE®

Unscramble these four Jumbles, one letter to
each square, to form four ordinary words.

LUMGO

TUGYO

LEWVIE

TESACK

WHAT SOME WEEKEND
GUESTS WEAR.

Now arrange the circled letters to form
the surprise answer, as suggested by the
above cartoon.

Print
answer
here ◯◯◯ **THEIR** ◯◯◯◯◯◯◯

JUMBLE®

Unscramble these four Jumbles, one letter to each square, to form four ordinary words.

DYPUG

LUSKK

POURRA

VELENE

WHAT A MAN WHOSE HAND IS QUICKER THAN THE EYE MIGHT GET.

Now arrange the circled letters to form the surprise answer, as suggested by the above cartoon.

Print answer here

JUMBLE®

Unscramble these four Jumbles, one letter to
each square, to form four ordinary words.

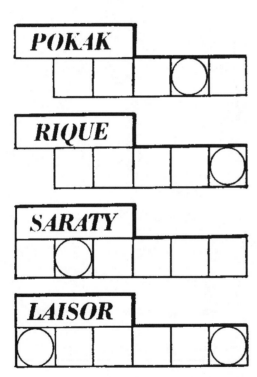

POKAK

RIQUE

SARATY

LAISOR

WHAT YOU CAN
EXPECT A DOZEN
ROSEBUDS TO
COME TO.

Now arrange the circled letters to form
the surprise answer, as suggested by the
above cartoon.

Print answer here ◯◯◯◯◯

JUMBLE®

Unscramble these four Jumbles, one letter to
each square, to form four ordinary words.

RESHE

WHASA

LOUBED

GIRDIF

WHAT ONE DEER
SAID ABOUT ANOTHER.

Now arrange the circled letters to form
the surprise answer, as suggested by the
above cartoon.

**Print
answer
here**   I ☐☐☐☐ I ☐☐☐ **HIS** ☐☐☐

71

JUMBLE®

Unscramble these four Jumbles, one letter to
each square, to form four ordinary words.

GLUBY

CUIJE

TEAREA

ROGDEC

WHAT A BRIGHT
GOLD DIGGER'S
WEAPON MIGHT BE.

Now arrange the circled letters to form
the surprise answer, as suggested by the
above cartoon.

Print answer here **HER** " ◯◯◯ – ◯◯◯ "

JUMBLE®

Unscramble these four Jumbles, one letter to
each square, to form four ordinary words.

ILFOO

GEBOF

NISSIT

PROWED

It looks like
my new system
will work

You might try
LOOKING for
work!

THE EASIEST
WAY TO MAKE
ENDS MEET.

Now arrange the circled letters to form
the surprise answer, as suggested by the
above cartoon.

*Print answer
here* ☐☐☐ ☐☐☐ **YOUR** ☐☐☐ !

73

JUMBLE®

Unscramble these four Jumbles, one letter to
each square, to form four ordinary words.

UNTOK

SMUCA

MANOSH

LAUBBE

A LIGHT KIND
OF BOOK.

Now arrange the circled letters to form
the surprise answer, as suggested by the
above cartoon.

Print answer here **A**

JUMBLE®

Unscramble these four Jumbles, one letter to
each square, to form four ordinary words.

LAIGY

BLAYM

YARAFF

FLUGEN

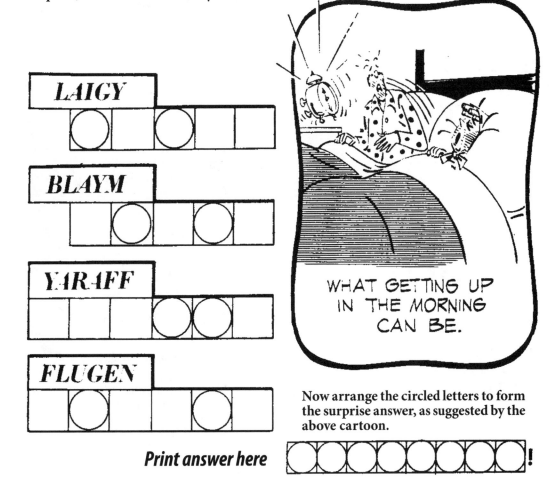

WHAT GETTING UP
IN THE MORNING
CAN BE.

Now arrange the circled letters to form
the surprise answer, as suggested by the
above cartoon.

Print answer here

⬡⬡⬡⬡⬡⬡⬡⬡⬡!

JUMBLE®

Unscramble these four Jumbles, one letter to
each square, to form four ordinary words.

GANYM

GUFEU

REDONP

BLIRME

WHAT MANY WHO FLY
FOR A LIVING WEAR.

Now arrange the circled letters to form
the surprise answer, as suggested by the
above cartoon.

Print answer here

JUMBLE®

Unscramble these four Jumbles, one letter to
each square, to form four ordinary words.

GYNIL

LABAN

URRUMM

ANSOOL

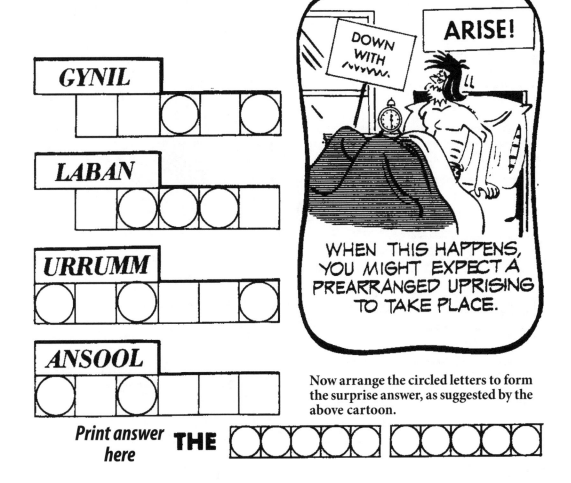

WHEN THIS HAPPENS,
YOU MIGHT EXPECT A
PREARRANGED UPRISING
TO TAKE PLACE.

Now arrange the circled letters to form
the surprise answer, as suggested by the
above cartoon.

**Print answer
here** **THE** ◯◯◯◯◯ ◯◯◯◯◯

JUMBLE®

Unscramble these four Jumbles, one letter to
each square, to form four ordinary words.

BATOU

SECAE

WYLLOH

CLARNE

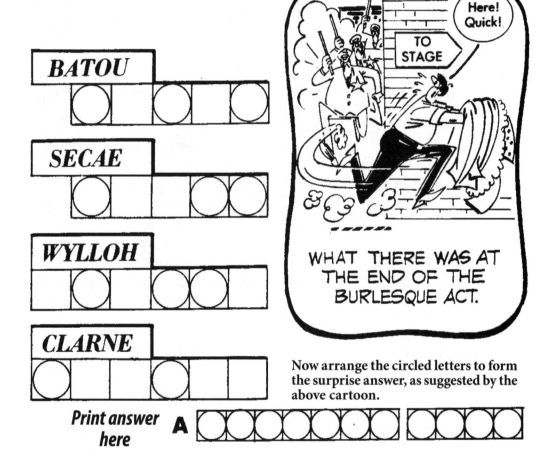

Here!
Quick!

TO
STAGE

WHAT THERE WAS AT
THE END OF THE
BURLESQUE ACT.

Now arrange the circled letters to form
the surprise answer, as suggested by the
above cartoon.

**Print answer
here** A

JUMBLE®

Unscramble these four Jumbles, one letter to
each square, to form four ordinary words.

NIFET

MYNEE

TRONIA

UMCAUV

WHEN YOU WANT TO
SLEEP THIS WAY,
BETTER PUT YOUR WATCH
UNDER YOUR PILLOW.

Now arrange the circled letters to form
the surprise answer, as suggested by the
above cartoon.

Print answer here " ◯◯◯◯ ◯◯◯◯ "

JUMBLE®

Unscramble these four Jumbles, one letter to
each square, to form four ordinary words.

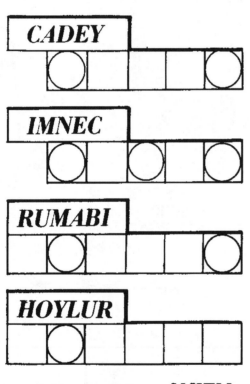

CADEY

IMNEC

RUMABI

HOYLUR

Ha! Ha! They think
we're crazy!!

Ha! Ha!

HOW HE PAID HIS
ASSISTANT.

Now arrange the circled letters to form
the surprise answer, as suggested by the
above cartoon.

Print answer here **WITH**

JUMBLE®

Unscramble these four Jumbles, one letter to
each square, to form four ordinary words.

YAKLE

NEETA

PRAMTE

ECTIPP

Where were you last night?

UP TO THE NECK IN
HOT WATER BUT
CONTINUES TO SING.

Now arrange the circled letters to form
the surprise answer, as suggested by the
above cartoon.

Print answer here **A**

PUZZLE
80

JUMBLE®

Unscramble these four Jumbles, one letter to each square, to form four ordinary words.

DEEGH

COSUR

DELMAT

SELUNS

And, if elected, I . . .

WHAT POLITICIANS WHO PROMISE PIE IN THE SKY OFTEN DO.

Now arrange the circled letters to form the surprise answer, as suggested by the above cartoon.

Print answer here ⬡⬡⬡ **YOUR** ⬡⬡⬡⬡⬡

JUMBLE®

Unscramble these four Jumbles, one letter to each square, to form four ordinary words.

ZALEH

NOBAT

SPYDOR

RADACE

My, you look GORGEOUS this morning, boss!

MAKE THIS AND YOU'RE ON THE WAY UP!

Now arrange the circled letters to form the surprise answer, as suggested by the above cartoon.

Print answer here **AN**

83

JUMBLE®

Unscramble these four Jumbles, one letter to
each square, to form four ordinary words.

DYSAN

WADAR

BOSULE

FROGLE

HOW SHE SOUNDED
WHEN SHE TRIED
TO SING HIGH C.

Now arrange the circled letters to form
the surprise answer, as suggested by the
above cartoon.

Print answer here " ☐☐☐ – ☐☐ "

JUMBLE®

Unscramble these four Jumbles, one letter to
each square, to form four ordinary words.

BIBAR

GELEY

KNABIG

DROBIF

THIS IS THE
BEST THING OUT!

Now arrange the circled letters to form
the surprise answer, as suggested by the
above cartoon.

Print answer here ◯ ◯◯◯◯

JUMBLE®

Unscramble these four Jumbles, one letter to each square, to form four ordinary words.

HIGEW

SYTTA

DIBEHN

NUCKOL

Hatching another culinary masterpiece?

WHY MOST THINGS DON'T HAVE TO BE THOUGHT OUT IN MODERN KITCHENS.

Now arrange the circled letters to form the surprise answer, as suggested by the above cartoon.

Print answer here   **THEY'RE** ◯◯◯◯◯◯◯ ◯◯◯

JUMBLE®

Unscramble these four Jumbles, one letter to
each square, to form four ordinary words.

GUNST

NOYGA

REHNID

WEEYAL

WHAT TO SAY WHEN
ASKED TO NAME THE
CAPITAL OF ALL
THE STATES.

Now arrange the circled letters to form
the surprise answer, as suggested by the
above cartoon.

Print answer here " ◯◯◯◯◯◯◯◯◯◯◯ "

JUMBLE®

Unscramble these four Jumbles, one letter to
each square, to form four ordinary words.

DACKE

YORRS

DECORF

ENCAME

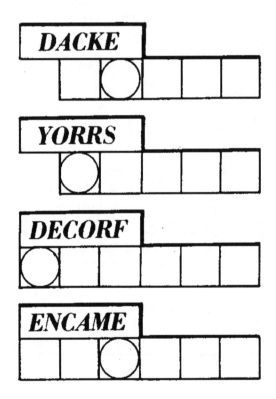

BECAUSE OF THIS
SOME MOVIE STARS
ARE "COOL."

Now arrange the circled letters to form
the surprise answer, as suggested by the
above cartoon.

Print answer here

JUMBLE®

Unscramble these four Jumbles, one letter to
each square, to form four ordinary words.

VOABE

NOWNK

NAPTIC

CIRNUH

ANYTHING? anything

WHAT A GIRL WHO SAYS
SHE'LL GO THROUGH
ANYTHING FOR A MAN
MIGHT HAVE IN MIND.

Now arrange the circled letters to form
the surprise answer, as suggested by the
above cartoon.

*Print answer
here*   **HIS**

89

JUMBLE®

Unscramble these four Jumbles, one letter to each square, to form four ordinary words.

LIMYK

YASES

LARPOR

MOFTEN

WHAT PEOPLE WHO DON'T SUMMER IN THE COUNTRY OFTEN DO IN THE CITY.

Now arrange the circled letters to form the surprise answer, as suggested by the above cartoon.

Print answer here

JUMBLE®

Unscramble these four Jumbles, one letter to each square, to form four ordinary words.

LAMDY

EXIDO

YURKET

DIBOLE

How'll
we get
home?

RACING

BURP!

A TEN-LETTER WORD THAT STARTS WITH G-A-S.

Now arrange the circled letters to form the surprise answer, as suggested by the above cartoon.

Print answer here

JUMBLE®

Unscramble these four Jumbles, one letter to
each square, to form four ordinary words.

CEENI

PROWE

DANNEC

YISMAL

Durn
revenooer!!

YOU CAN MAKE THIS
BUT YOU'LL NEVER
LIVE TO SEE IT!

Now arrange the circled letters to form
the surprise answer, as suggested by the
above cartoon.

Print answer here

JUMBLE®

Unscramble these four Jumbles, one letter to
each square, to form four ordinary words.

BORNI

TULFE

REPIME

SOLFIS

Careful!

WHERE YOU HAVE
MOUNTAIN RANGES YOU
MIGHT ALSO FIND THIS.

Now arrange the circled letters to form
the surprise answer, as suggested by the
above cartoon.

Print answer here 〇〇〇〇〇〇 〇〇〇〇〇

93

JUMBLE®

Unscramble these four Jumbles, one letter to each square, to form four ordinary words.

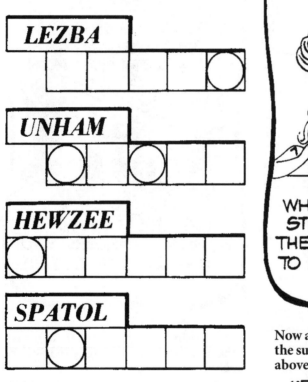

LEZBA

UNHAM

HEWZEE

SPATOL

Parts of Speech

WHAT THE INATTENTIVE STUDENT SAID WHEN THE TEACHER ASKED HIM TO NAME TWO PRONOUNS.

Now arrange the circled letters to form the surprise answer, as suggested by the above cartoon.

Print answer here  , ?"

JUMBLE®

Unscramble these four Jumbles, one letter to
each square, to form four ordinary words.

PARPE

KONET

LYNFOD

VISTEN

WHAT THE GOSSIP WAS.

Now arrange the circled letters to form
the surprise answer, as suggested by the
above cartoon.

Print
answer
here

THE " ⬡⬡⬡⬡⬡ " OF THE ⬡⬡⬡⬡⬡

JUMBLE®

Unscramble these four Jumbles, one letter to
each square, to form four ordinary words.

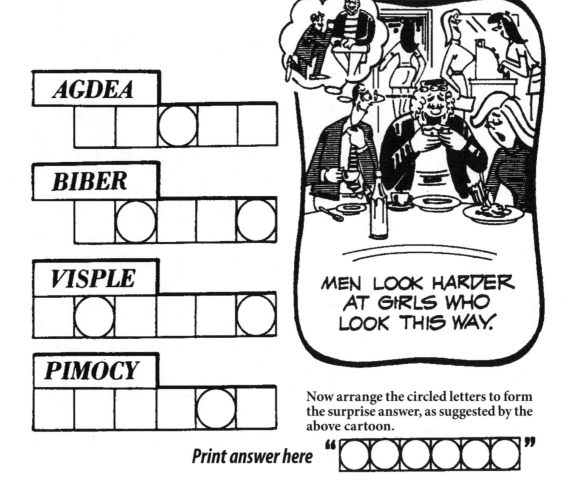

AGDEA

BIBER

VISPLE

PIMOCY

MEN LOOK HARDER
AT GIRLS WHO
LOOK THIS WAY.

Now arrange the circled letters to form
the surprise answer, as suggested by the
above cartoon.

Print answer here " ⟨◯◯◯◯◯◯⟩ "

JUMBLE®

Unscramble these four Jumbles, one letter to
each square, to form four ordinary words.

YORFE

VENAK

YAXLAG

ENBOAM

WHAT A TAXPAYER
HOPES FOR.

Now arrange the circled letters to form
the surprise answer, as suggested by the
above cartoon.

*Print answer
here* A ⬡⬡⬡⬡⬡ IN THE ⬡⬡⬡⬡

JUMBLE®

Unscramble these four Jumbles, one letter to
each square, to form four ordinary words.

TRYAR

KORPE

TEABED

GREATY

OFTEN CHARGED FOR
BETTER SERVICE.

Now arrange the circled letters to form
the surprise answer, as suggested by the
above cartoon.

Print answer here **A**

JUMBLE®

Unscramble these four Jumbles, one letter to each square, to form four ordinary words.

SOPIE

ORRGI

REMMAH

ENGOUT

When do the trained horses come on?

WHAT THE BOXING CHAMP TURNED CIRCUS PERFORMER BECAME.

Now arrange the circled letters to form the surprise answer, as suggested by the above cartoon.

Print answer here

JUMBLE®

Unscramble these four Jumbles, one letter to
each square, to form four ordinary words.

BIELL

AMMAD

NOPHTY

DEFUAL

I'll be late
for school if
I come back

SERVES TO HOLD
IMPORTANT THINGS UP.

Now arrange the circled letters to form
the surprise answer, as suggested by the
above cartoon.

Print answer here **A**

JUMBLE®

Unscramble these four Jumbles, one letter to
each square, to form four ordinary words.

NEPOR

TAXEC

YIHRTT

LAYGEL

Escaped!

ANIMALS YOU MIGHT
FIND ON THE
GOLF COURSE.

Now arrange the circled letters to form
the surprise answer, as suggested by the
above cartoon.

Print answer here

JUMBLE®

Unscramble these four Jumbles, one letter to each square, to form four ordinary words.

YINCC

ROLYG

NIDIOE

HUMBAS

HOW A GUY WHO STARTS THE DAY WITH AN "EYE-OPENER" MIGHT END UP.

Now arrange the circled letters to form the surprise answer, as suggested by the above cartoon.

Print answer here " ◯◯◯◯◯ "

JUMBLE®

Unscramble these four Jumbles, one letter to each square, to form four ordinary words.

VEREF

KLIMY

NEURED

ENCOBA

A watercress sandwich, please

GOULASH.... $1.30
ROAST BEEF . $1.35
CUTLET...... $1.25
PORK CHOPS. $1.30

WHEN A PERSON'S THIS, YOU WOULDN'T EXPECT HIM TO BE A VEGETARIAN.

Now arrange the circled letters to form the surprise answer, as suggested by the above cartoon.

Print answer here ⭕⭕⭕⭕⭕

JUMBLE®

Unscramble these four Jumbles, one letter to each square, to form four ordinary words.

DOPET

YEHRM

SURIAD

RUIPFY

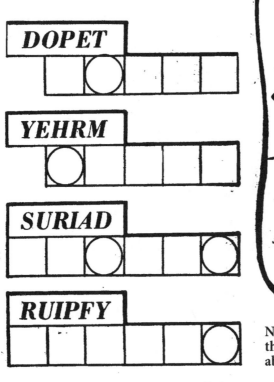

Tee hee! He's so bashful!

CLEANERS

THESE PEOPLE OFTEN CHANGE COLOR.

Now arrange the circled letters to form the surprise answer, as suggested by the above cartoon.

Print answer here

JUMBLE®

Unscramble these four Jumbles, one letter to each square, to form four ordinary words.

YUNTT

NULGE

ERWANS

SINOUF

Let's go!

MIGHT HELP OVERCOME DIFFICULTIES WITH BOTTLENECKS.

Now arrange the circled letters to form the surprise answer, as suggested by the above cartoon.

Print answer here **A** ⬡⬡⬡⬡⬡⬡⬡

JUMBLE®

Unscramble these four Jumbles, one letter to
each square, to form four ordinary words.

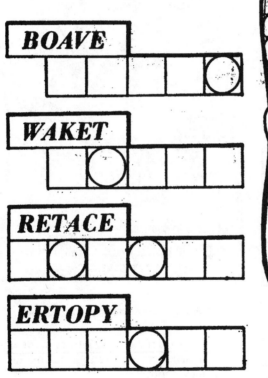

BOAVE

WAKET

RETACE

ERTOPY

ISLAND SURROUNDINGS.

Now arrange the circled letters to form
the surprise answer, as suggested by the
above cartoon.

Print answer here

JUMBLE®

Unscramble these four Jumbles, one letter to
each square, to form four ordinary words.

YAHNE

RAOAM

BOBJER

HARTTO

This man's mine!

He belongs to her?

WHAT SHE CALLED
HER BOYFRIEND.

Now arrange the circled letters to form
the surprise answer, as suggested by the
above cartoon.

Print answer here

JUMBLE®

Unscramble these four Jumbles, one letter to each square, to form four ordinary words.

SOGEO

TYFFA

NURYGH

FLUFEM

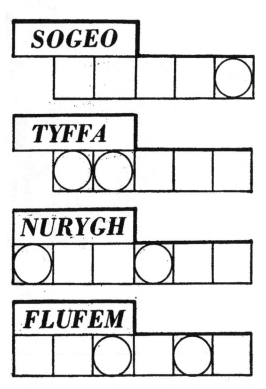

HELD UP—AT A PUBLIC MEETING!

Now arrange the circled letters to form the surprise answer, as suggested by the above cartoon.

Print answer here

JUMBLE®

Unscramble these four Jumbles, one letter to
each square, to form four ordinary words.

UGIED

COHLT

CORTER

LIMSAD

WHAT THEY WERE
AFTER BEING LICKED.

Now arrange the circled letters to form
the surprise answer, as suggested by the
above cartoon.

Print answer here

JUMBLE®

Unscramble these four Jumbles, one letter to
each square, to form four ordinary words.

VALIE

SHOWE

DOSPYR

REKALT

Right!

Wrong!

WE'RE NOT SURE

?

YOU CAN'T DO IT IN THE MIDDLE.

Now arrange the circled letters to form
the surprise answer, as suggested by the
above cartoon.

Print answer here

JUMBLE®

Unscramble these four Jumbles, one letter to
each square, to form four ordinary words.

THOOP

HIWGE

PRULAB

PUNCKA

Behave or I'll
spank you!

DOG
RACES

YOU WOULDN'T WANT
TO HURT THIS LITTLE
DOG BUT SOUNDS
LIKE IT.

Now arrange the circled letters to form
the surprise answer, as suggested by the
above cartoon.

Print answer here   A "◯◯◯◯-◯◯◯"

JUMBLE®

Unscramble these four Jumbles, one letter to
each square, to form four ordinary words.

HILEW

VAINE

CEDROF

NITIVE

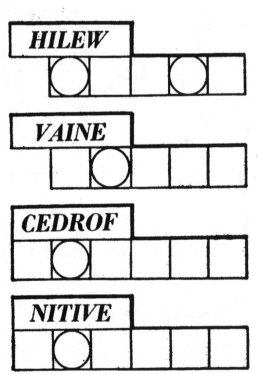

Stop
that
hooting!

SAVE ON
NIGHTTIME
RATES

COULD BE WISE—
TO FLY AT NIGHT.

Now arrange the circled letters to form
the surprise answer, as suggested by the
above cartoon.

Print answer here

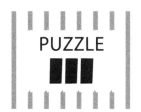
JUMBLE®

Unscramble these four Jumbles, one letter to
each square, to form four ordinary words.

RENIL

LAGIE

TEENAB

MURTES

SOMETIMES SHIVERS
AT MEALTIME.

Now arrange the circled letters to form
the surprise answer, as suggested by the
above cartoon.

Print answer here

113

JUMBLE®

Unscramble these four Jumbles, one letter to each square, to form four ordinary words.

ANCOP

VATLE

CIANAM

FRIVED

Everything O.K. now?

MARRIAGE COUNSELOR

Yes!

PEOPLE IN COMPLETE AGREEMENT MAY SPEAK WITH ONE—

Now arrange the circled letters to form the surprise answer, as suggested by the above cartoon.

Print answer here ☐☐☐☐☐

114

JUMBLE®

Unscramble these four Jumbles, one letter to each square, to form four ordinary words.

BLEER

URPPE

PLOARE

RYLURF

MADE TO MEASURE.

Now arrange the circled letters to form the surprise answer, as suggested by the above cartoon.

Print answer here **A** ⬡⬡⬡⬡⬡⬡

JUMBLE®

Unscramble these four Jumbles, one letter to
each square, to form four ordinary words.

NIGLY

TINFE

INDIGH

DEGULC

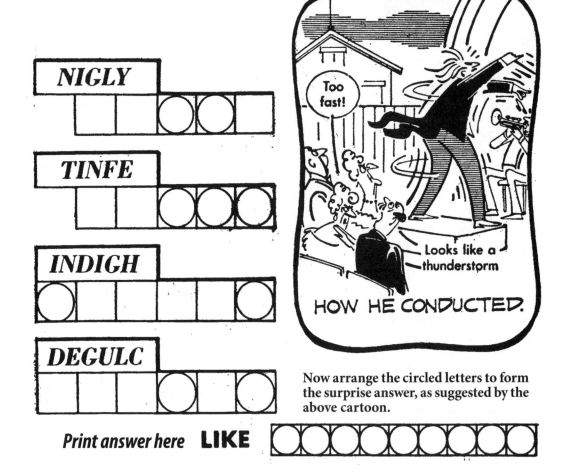

Too fast!

Looks like a thunderstorm

HOW HE CONDUCTED.

Now arrange the circled letters to form
the surprise answer, as suggested by the
above cartoon.

Print answer here **LIKE** ⬡⬡⬡⬡⬡⬡⬡⬡⬡⬡

116

JUMBLE®

Unscramble these four Jumbles, one letter to
each square, to form four ordinary words.

VURCE

TOAPI

RUQRAY

HOKERS

USED FOR
AN OPENING.

Now arrange the circled letters to form
the surprise answer, as suggested by the
above cartoon.

Print answer here

117

JUMBLE®

Unscramble these four Jumbles, one letter to each square, to form four ordinary words.

TAIMY

FYTHE

UPGALE

NISSIT

FOOD THAT MAKES APES TIGHT.

Now arrange the circled letters to form the surprise answer, as suggested by the above cartoon.

Print answer here

118

JUMBLE®

Unscramble these four Jumbles, one letter to
each square, to form four ordinary words.

TROIB

FIMOT

REPUMB

ONNACY

I don't know which is worse

COULD BE TWO
CATS MAKING SOUNDS
LIKE A DRUM.

Now arrange the circled letters to form
the surprise answer, as suggested by the
above cartoon.

Print answer here "◯◯◯ – ◯◯◯"

JUMBLE.

Unscramble these four Jumbles, one letter to
each square, to form four ordinary words.

HAWSS

PLIMB

GUNJEL

RUPPLE

Ya mean
they ain't
pointin' at
nothin'?

WHAT SHOOTING
ANYWHERE MIGHT BE.

Now arrange the circled letters to form
the surprise answer, as suggested by the
above cartoon.

Print answer here

JUMBLE®

Unscramble these four Jumbles, one letter to
each square, to form four ordinary words.

NOILG

LYRDY

DISMOW

INVOIS

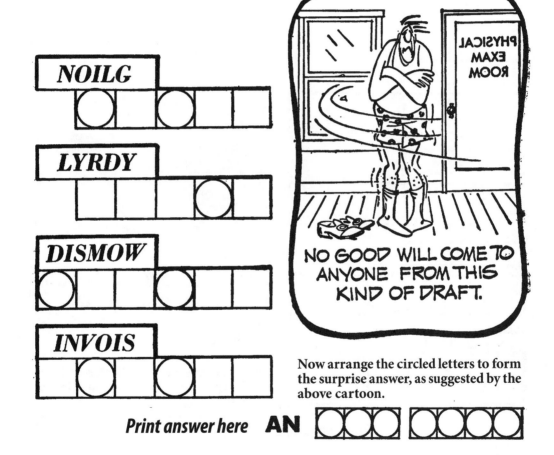

NO GOOD WILL COME TO
ANYONE FROM THIS
KIND OF DRAFT.

PHYSICAL
EXAM
ROOM

Now arrange the circled letters to form
the surprise answer, as suggested by the
above cartoon.

Print answer here **AN** ☐☐☐ ☐☐☐☐☐

121

JUMBLE®

Unscramble these four Jumbles, one letter to each square, to form four ordinary words.

FRUOM

DEACK

REPERF

CROONB

THIS BLOW WAS GOT FROM A SCUFFLE.

Now arrange the circled letters to form the surprise answer, as suggested by the above cartoon.

Print answer here ◯ "◯◯◯◯◯"

JUMBLE®

Unscramble these four Jumbles, one letter to
each square, to form four ordinary words.

LAHCK

HEGIT

TEVVLE

RUNUTE

None better
exist

ONE—THAT MIGHT BE
WORTH MORE THAN ANY
OF THE OTHERS.

Now arrange the circled letters to form
the surprise answer, as suggested by the
above cartoon.

Print answer here

JUMBLE®

Unscramble these four Jumbles, one letter to
each square, to form four ordinary words.

ANKEW

NAISE

KUBECT

GROUME

AMERICAN
LITERATURE

SWEDEN FINLAND
NORWAY
DENMARK
NORTH
SEA

CHIEF LIBRARIAN

A FINN HELPED HIM
TO BECOME FAMOUS.

Now arrange the circled letters to form
the surprise answer, as suggested by the
above cartoon.

Print answer here

JUMBLE®

Unscramble these four Jumbles, one letter to
each square, to form four ordinary words.

HASAW

ROFAL

NOAWHY

LENKEN

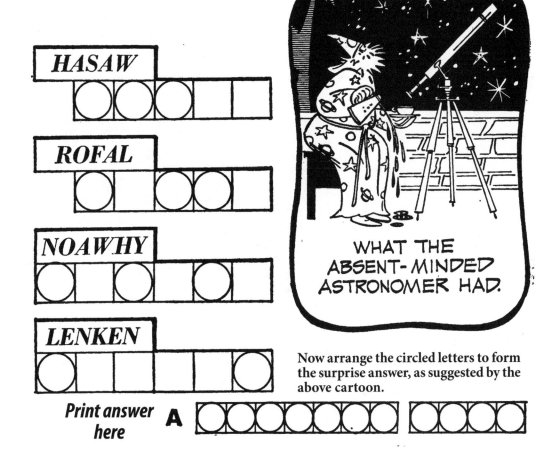

WHAT THE
ABSENT-MINDED
ASTRONOMER HAD.

Now arrange the circled letters to form
the surprise answer, as suggested by the
above cartoon.

Print answer
here **A**

JUMBLE®

Unscramble these four Jumbles, one letter to
each square, to form four ordinary words.

CETTO

HOUGD

TUFLAR

PENXED

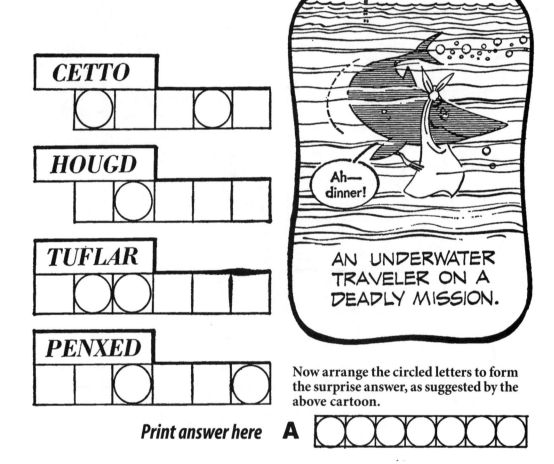

Ah—
dinner!

AN UNDERWATER
TRAVELER ON A
DEADLY MISSION.

Now arrange the circled letters to form
the surprise answer, as suggested by the
above cartoon.

Print answer here **A**

126

JUMBLE®

Unscramble these four Jumbles, one letter to
each square, to form four ordinary words.

IDDEC

NOGGI

CENNAD

MOHFAT

SOUND AS A BELL!

Now arrange the circled letters to form
the surprise answer, as suggested by the
above cartoon.

Print answer here ◯◯◯◯◯◯◯◯◯

JUMBLE®

Unscramble these four Jumbles, one letter to
each square, to form four ordinary words.

USEAT

TRIDY

INSEPP

FUSULE

DAMSELS APPEALED
TO KNIGHTS OF OLD
IN THIS.

Now arrange the circled letters to form
the surprise answer, as suggested by the
above cartoon.

Print answer here

JUMBLE®

Unscramble these four Jumbles, one letter to each square, to form four ordinary words.

TYTID

YABBE

INLOOT

AGCUTH

I feel like leaving

Shh! It's just starting!

WHAT TO DO AFTER THE OVERTURE.

Now arrange the circled letters to form the surprise answer, as suggested by the above cartoon.

Print answer here

JUMBLE®

Unscramble these four Jumbles, one letter to
each square, to form four ordinary words.

JEECT

HAKSY

LAMTEL

YAWTER

THIS DIRECTION MIGHT
CAUSE AGITATION.

Now arrange the circled letters to form
the surprise answer, as suggested by the
above cartoon.

Print answer here " ⬡⬡⬡⬡⬡⬡ ⬡⬡⬡⬡ "

JUMBLE®

Unscramble these four Jumbles, one letter to
each square, to form four ordinary words.

GAADE

SWEYN

NOMMOC

IMUSSE

Safety?

WHERE TO GET
MARRIED IN
SCANDINAVIA.

Now arrange the circled letters to form
the surprise answer, as suggested by the
above cartoon.

Print answer here " ☐ - ☐☐☐ - ☐☐ "

131

JUMBLE®

Unscramble these four Jumbles, one letter to
each square, to form four ordinary words.

YIRLC

HOPUC

LIMBEN

RALCOR

Bread and
water!

It'll simmer
you down!

THIS JAIL DOESN'T
SOUND SO HOT.

Now arrange the circled letters to form
the surprise answer, as suggested by the
above cartoon.

Print answer here **THE** ◯◯◯◯◯◯◯

JUMBLE®

Unscramble these four Jumbles, one letter to
each square, to form four ordinary words.

NELLK

GAANP

LANARC

VUSSER

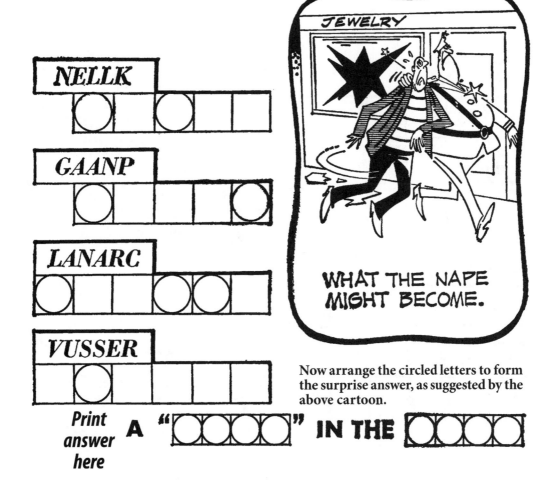

WHAT THE NAPE
MIGHT BECOME.

Now arrange the circled letters to form
the surprise answer, as suggested by the
above cartoon.

Print
answer
here   A "⭕⭕⭕⭕⭕" IN THE ⭕⭕⭕⭕

JUMBLE®

Unscramble these four Jumbles, one letter to
each square, to form four ordinary words.

SEUDO

PYTEM

HEHRST

MAHNLY

There
There
TAILOR

HOW TO GET RID
OF TEARS.

Now arrange the circled letters to form
the surprise answer, as suggested by the
above cartoon.

Print answer here

134

JUMBLE®

Unscramble these four Jumbles, one letter to
each square, to form four ordinary words.

YALFE

SONDY

GAMADE

DURSTY

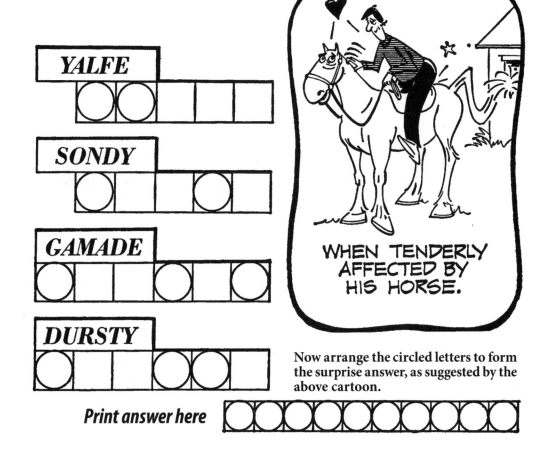

WHEN TENDERLY
AFFECTED BY
HIS HORSE.

Now arrange the circled letters to form
the surprise answer, as suggested by the
above cartoon.

Print answer here

JUMBLE®

Unscramble these four Jumbles, one letter to
each square, to form four ordinary words.

KWONN

YAWNT

COLLEA

GYSSAR

HOW SHE FOUND A
SHOE TO FIT.

Now arrange the circled letters to form
the surprise answer, as suggested by the
above cartoon.

Print answer here **AT** ⟨ ⟩⟨ ⟩⟨ ⟩⟨ ⟩ ⟨ ⟩⟨ ⟩⟨ ⟩⟨ ⟩

JUMBLE®

Unscramble these four Jumbles, one letter to
each square, to form four ordinary words.

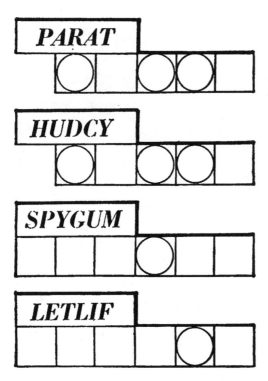

PARAT

HUDCY

SPYGUM

LETLIF

Means
a lot of
hard work

HE SAID THIS WAS
THE ACTING GAME!

Now arrange the circled letters to form
the surprise answer, as suggested by the
above cartoon.

Print answer here

137

JUMBLE®

Unscramble these four Jumbles, one letter to
each square, to form four ordinary words.

ROGIN

BATHI

DORPAY

MUGNIP

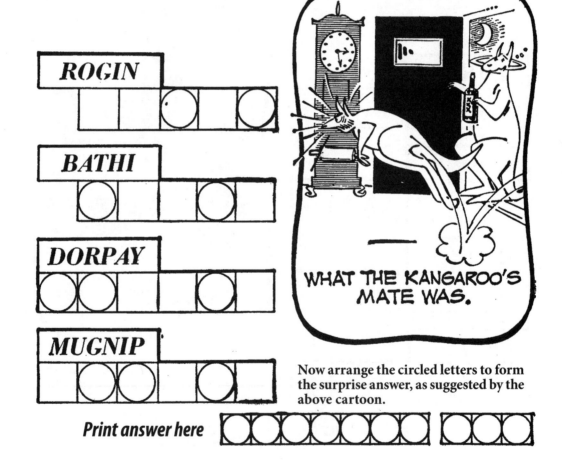

WHAT THE KANGAROO'S
MATE WAS.

Now arrange the circled letters to form
the surprise answer, as suggested by the
above cartoon.

Print answer here

138

JUMBLE®

Unscramble these four Jumbles, one letter to
each square, to form four ordinary words.

DABIE

VIRTE

RIDOLF

APITOE

No!

Yes!

WHY THE BLOND
SEEMED MORE
REASONABLE.

Now arrange the circled letters to form
the surprise answer, as suggested by the
above cartoon.

Print answer here **SHE WAS**

JUMBLE®

Unscramble these four Jumbles, one letter to
each square, to form four ordinary words.

SIDAY

GRUPE

DIPTUN

INFURA

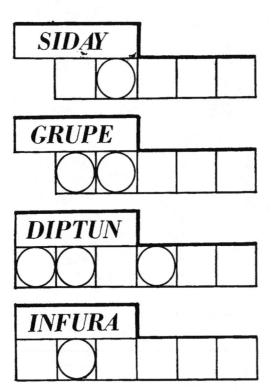

He's frank,
honest and
sincere

ON THIS YOU SHOULD
GET TO THE TOP.

Now arrange the circled letters to form
the surprise answer, as suggested by the
above cartoon.

Print answer here **THE**

JUMBLE®

Unscramble these four Jumbles, one letter to
each square, to form four ordinary words.

BUDOT

RAPOE

VALNYS

ASOURE

SUPPORT AN
OLD-FASHIONED
RESTING PLACE.

Now arrange the circled letters to form
the surprise answer, as suggested by the
above cartoon.

Print answer here

JUMBLE®

Unscramble these four Jumbles, one letter to
each square, to form four ordinary words.

CLATH·

VINGE

DEECIV

AUGIAN

Ten farthings,
please

I'll give
you five

BREW

NEVER TRY TO DO
THIS WITH A WITCH.

Now arrange the circled letters to form
the surprise answer, as suggested by the
above cartoon.

Print answer here "◯◯◯-◯◯◯"

JUMBLE®

Unscramble these four Jumbles, one letter to
each square, to form four ordinary words.

BREYD

LAANB

TRIEHD

ARQUEV

WHAT WAS THE
OUTCOME OF ALL
THAT ACTIVITY
AT THE BREWERY?

Now arrange the circled letters to form
the surprise answer, as suggested by the
above cartoon.

Print answer here

JUMBLE®

Unscramble these four Jumbles, one letter to
each square, to form four ordinary words.

REWAY

POCUR

TENDAL

DRAZIL

Some other
day

Start with
the lawn!

THIS LIQUID
CAN CAUSE PLANS
TO CHANGE.

Now arrange the circled letters to form
the surprise answer, as suggested by the
above cartoon.

Print answer here

JUMBLE®

Unscramble these four Jumbles, one letter to
each square, to form four ordinary words.

YARDT

REVNY

CLOSIA

UNTOAM

Off
with
their
heads!

WHAT THE END OF
THE DYNASTY WAS.

Now arrange the circled letters to form
the surprise answer, as suggested by the
above cartoon.

Print answer here

145

JUMBLE®

Unscramble these four Jumbles, one letter to each square, to form four ordinary words.

KOWEA

NUTED

RAWTIE

FRAGEO

Now arrange the circled letters to form the surprise answer, as suggested by the above cartoon.

Print answer here ⬡⬡⬡ ⬡⬡⬡ ⬡⬡⬡

146

JUMBLE®

Unscramble these four Jumbles, one letter to
each square, to form four ordinary words.

TULSY

NAHDY

CLINAG

NEMPAN

WHAT WORKING IN
THE NURSERY WAS
FOR THE GARDENER.

Now arrange the circled letters to form
the surprise answer, as suggested by the
above cartoon.

Print answer here "◯◯◯◯◯' ◯ ◯◯◯◯"

JUMBLE®

Unscramble these four Jumbles, one letter to
each square, to form four ordinary words.

RAFIE

KALEF

DRATOW

MEBBUN

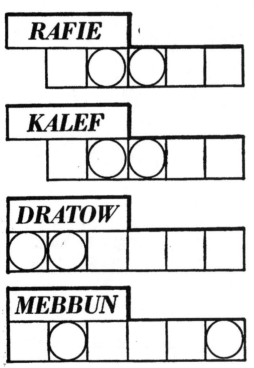

Sells 'em and
puts all his
money in
the bank

THIS KIND OF CRAFT
HELPS ONE TO SAVE.

Now arrange the circled letters to form
the surprise answer, as suggested by the
above cartoon.

Print answer here **A**

JUMBLE®

Unscramble these four Jumbles, one letter to
each square, to form four ordinary words.

TILIM

YUMMG

DEGUBB

PARTIE

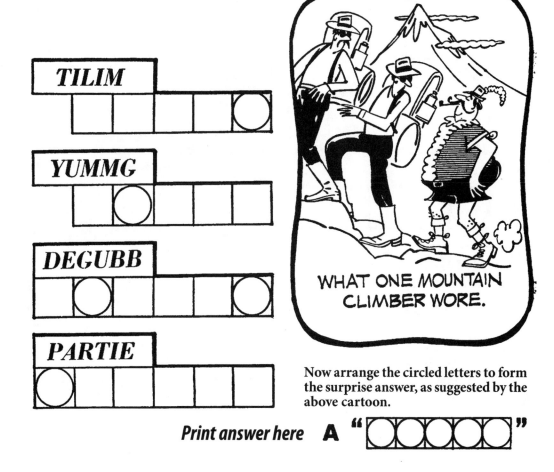

WHAT ONE MOUNTAIN
CLIMBER WORE.

Now arrange the circled letters to form
the surprise answer, as suggested by the
above cartoon.

Print answer here **A** " ⬡⬡⬡⬡⬡ "

JUMBLE®

Unscramble these four Jumbles, one letter to each square, to form four ordinary words.

INVEX

VARFO

ENBARN

PINTUR

Wow! I'm rich!

And he paid practically nothing for them!

BIG MONEY— FOR A SONG!

Now arrange the circled letters to form the surprise answer, as suggested by the above cartoon.

Print answer here " ◯◯◯ – ◯◯◯◯ "

JUMBLE®

Unscramble these four Jumbles, one letter to
each square, to form four ordinary words.

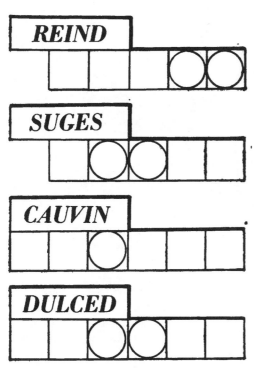

REIND

SUGES

CAUVIN

DULCED

CIRCUMSTANCES IN
WHICH YOU MIGHT FIND
YOURSELF AFTER GOING
TO ONE OF THOSE
EXPENSIVE HEALTH SPAS.

Now arrange the circled letters to form
the surprise answer, as suggested by the
above cartoon.

Print answer here " "

JUMBLE®

Unscramble these four Jumbles, one letter to
each square, to form four ordinary words.

SAREE

YORIN

CAPELA

MULVLE

THEY OFTEN GO OUT
TO SEA AT PORTS.

Now arrange the circled letters to form
the surprise answer, as suggested by the
above cartoon.

Print answer here

JUMBLE®

Unscramble these four Jumbles, one letter to
each square, to form four ordinary words.

VAMUE

ETTEW

REBARL

ZIGAHN

Losing another
day's salary!

Docked?

IT DOESN'T PAY
HIM TO PLAY!

Now arrange the circled letters to form
the surprise answer, as suggested by the
above cartoon.

Print answer here **AN** ⭕⭕⭕⭕⭕⭕⭕

JUMBLE®

Unscramble these four Jumbles, one letter to
each square, to form four ordinary words.

CENOU

ORVAB

FARREY

TECKOP

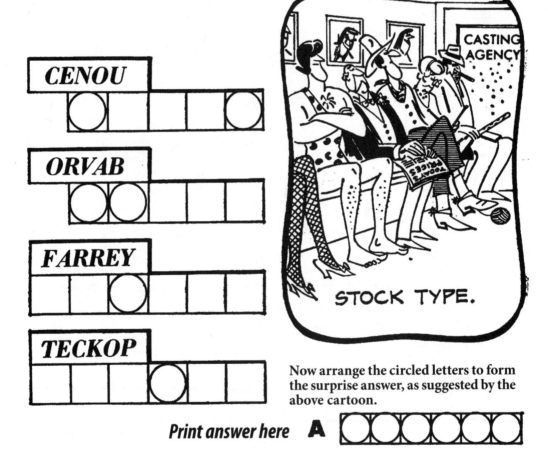

CASTING
AGENCY

STOCK TYPE.

Now arrange the circled letters to form
the surprise answer, as suggested by the
above cartoon.

Print answer here **A** ⬡⬡⬡⬡⬡⬡⬡

JUMBLE®

Unscramble these four Jumbles, one letter to
each square, to form four ordinary words.

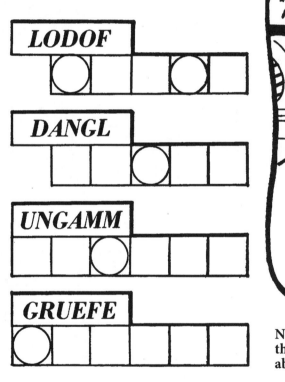

LODOF

DANGL

UNGAMM

GRUEFE

It's the end!

IN YOUR THROAT,
BUT DON'T WORRY—
YOU WON'T CROAK!

Now arrange the circled letters to form
the surprise answer, as suggested by the
above cartoon.

Print answer here

JUMBLE®

Unscramble these four Jumbles, one letter to
each square, to form four ordinary words.

LOVEN

MENGO

BORREB

WALLUF

Vacation over already?

WHAT SHORTS
MAY NOT BE.

Now arrange the circled letters to form
the surprise answer, as suggested by the
above cartoon.

Print answer here ⬡⬡⬡⬡ **FOR** ⬡⬡⬡⬡

JUMBLE®

Unscramble these four Jumbles, one letter to
each square, to form four ordinary words.

ORFEC

THYIC

BELEEF

PONCAY

TO THE BALL GAME......

Ball!

HE SANG AS
HE PLAYED.

Now arrange the circled letters to form
the surprise answer, as suggested by the
above cartoon.

Print answer here

157

JUMBLE®

Unscramble these four Jumbles, one letter to each square, to form four ordinary words.

WARLD

OUMID

PANPHE

TREENI

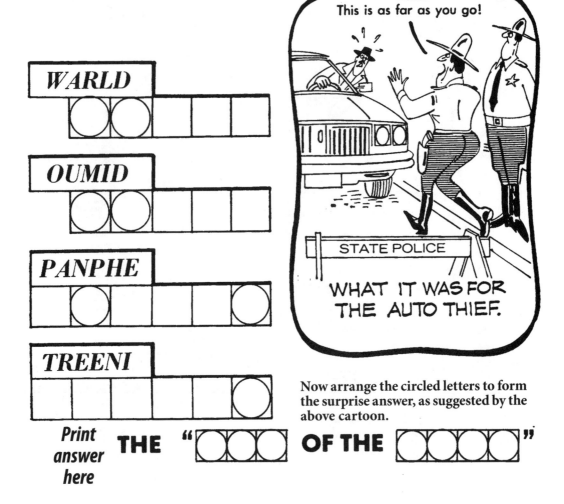

This is as far as you go!

STATE POLICE

WHAT IT WAS FOR THE AUTO THIEF.

Now arrange the circled letters to form the surprise answer, as suggested by the above cartoon.

Print answer here

THE " ◯◯◯ OF THE ◯◯◯◯ "

JUMBLE®

Unscramble these four Jumbles, one letter to
each square, to form four ordinary words.

HOLLE

ATTIR

GROITE

NAITED

We'll get
you there

IF YOU'RE ON IT ·
YOU'LL BE ON TIME.

Now arrange the circled letters to form
the surprise answer, as suggested by the
above cartoon.

Print answer here ☐☐☐ ☐☐☐

JUMBLE®

Unscramble these four Jumbles, one letter to
each square, to form four ordinary words.

ENVIL

STOFI

VAINED

TRAUGI

TAKEN UNAWARES.

Now arrange the circled letters to form
the surprise answer, as suggested by the
above cartoon.

Print answer here

JUMBLE.

Unscramble these four Jumbles, one letter to
each square, to form four ordinary words.

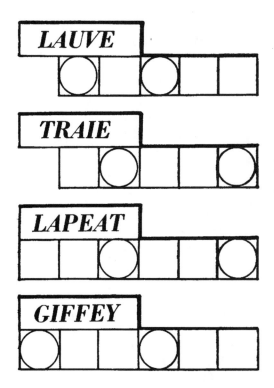

LAUVE

TRAIE

LAPEAT

GIFFEY

Three-
day
passes
for
everyone!

HAS A ROUSING
EFFECT ON
SERVICEMEN.

Now arrange the circled letters to form
the surprise answer, as suggested by the
above cartoon.

Print answer here

JUMBLE®

Unscramble these four Jumbles, one letter to each square, to form four ordinary words.

SELBS

WODDY

REJESY

UNBOAD

THE LAST THING
THE BRIDE
PROMISED TO DO.

Now arrange the circled letters to form
the surprise answer, as suggested by the
above cartoon.

Print answer here " ◯◯◯◯ "

JUMBLE®

JAILBREAK

Challenger Puzzles

JUMBLE.

Unscramble these six Jumbles, one letter to each square, to form six ordinary words.

RICKYT

ONABBO

MOVULE

DIMPOU

NARTTY

LAWVOA

WHAT THE REFORMED BACHELOR SAID HIS LIFE NOW WAS.

Now arrange the circled letters to form the surprise answer, as suggested by the above cartoon.

Print answer here ⬡⬡ ⬡⬡⬡⬡ ⬡⬡⬡⬡

JUMBLE®

Unscramble these six Jumbles, one letter to
each square, to form six ordinary words.

YESGER

NUCHEQ

WOCALL

CUSTOC

VAHLED

TOBUNT

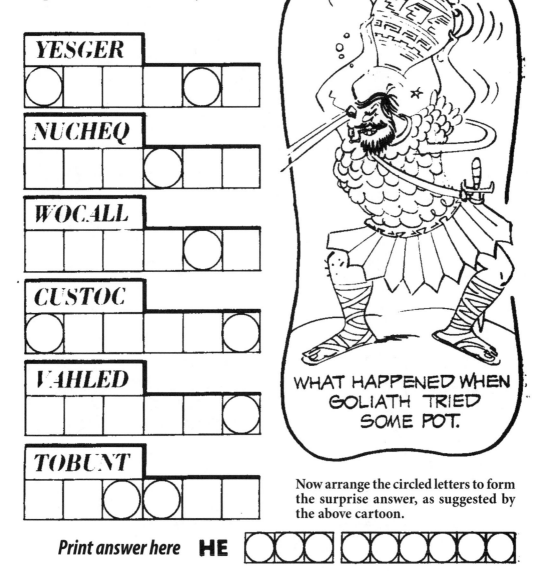

WHAT HAPPENED WHEN
GOLIATH TRIED
SOME POT.

Now arrange the circled letters to form
the surprise answer, as suggested by
the above cartoon.

Print answer here **HE** ☐◯◯◯ ◯◯◯◯◯◯◯☐

JUMBLE®

Unscramble these six Jumbles, one letter to
each square, to form six ordinary words.

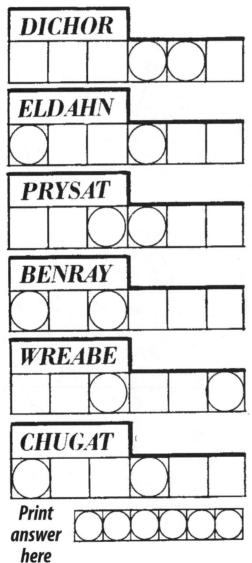

DICHOR

ELDAHN

PRYSAT

BENRAY

WREABE

CHUGAT

This
ought
to do
it!

MT. EVEREST
SUMMIT

WHAT SOME PEOPLE
GO TO GREAT
LENGTHS TO DO.

Now arrange the circled letters to form
the surprise answer, as suggested by
the above cartoon.

**Print
answer
here** ⬡⬡⬡⬡⬡⬡ **THEIR** ⬡⬡⬡⬡⬡⬡

JUMBLE®

Unscramble these six Jumbles, one letter to
each square, to form six ordinary words.

ARPITE

KOECIO

SILENE

TINBAD

LURTIA

GRENED

41 . . . 23 . . . 37 . . .

Like
WOW!

THESE ARE OFTEN
SENSATIONAL AT A
BEAUTY CONTEST.

Now arrange the circled letters to form
the surprise answer, as suggested by
the above cartoon.

*Print
answer
here*

167

JUMBLE®

Unscramble these six Jumbles, one letter to each square, to form six ordinary words.

LAYREY

STIGED

MEETOL

GANTEM

TAIREW

PARPEA

1970

46 . . .
47 . . .
48 . . .

WHAT 1969 PENNIES ARE WORTH THIS YEAR.

Now arrange the circled letters to form the surprise answer, as suggested by the above cartoon.

Print answer here

ALMOST

JUMBLE.

Unscramble these six Jumbles, one letter to each square, to form six ordinary words.

FLAHBE

REVORF

GAMIPE

RAHDLE

YUNASE

LEPPUR

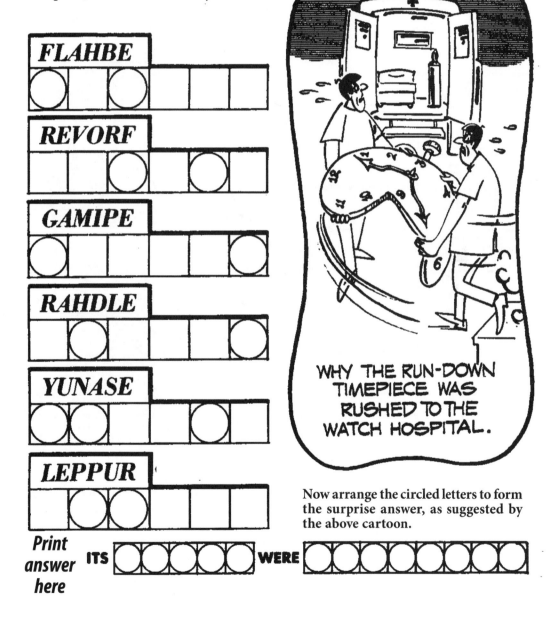

WHY THE RUN-DOWN
TIMEPIECE WAS
RUSHED TO THE
WATCH HOSPITAL.

Now arrange the circled letters to form the surprise answer, as suggested by the above cartoon.

Print
answer
here

ITS ⬡⬡⬡⬡⬡ WERE ⬡⬡⬡⬡⬡⬡⬡⬡⬡

JUMBLE®

Unscramble these six Jumbles, one letter to
each square, to form six ordinary words.

MORRET

THARRE

FIELDE

VINTER

BELMAG

NALLEF

HOW THE BRIGHT
ROOKIE WAS
SIGNED UP.

Now arrange the circled letters to form
the surprise answer, as suggested by
the above cartoon.

*Print answer
here* ⬡⬡⬡⬡⬡ ⬡⬡⬡ **THE** ⬡⬡⬡

JUMBLE®

Unscramble these six Jumbles, one letter to each square, to form six ordinary words.

YUPRIF

STAFIE

CRYGLE

SENNIG

WOBETS

GESTAK

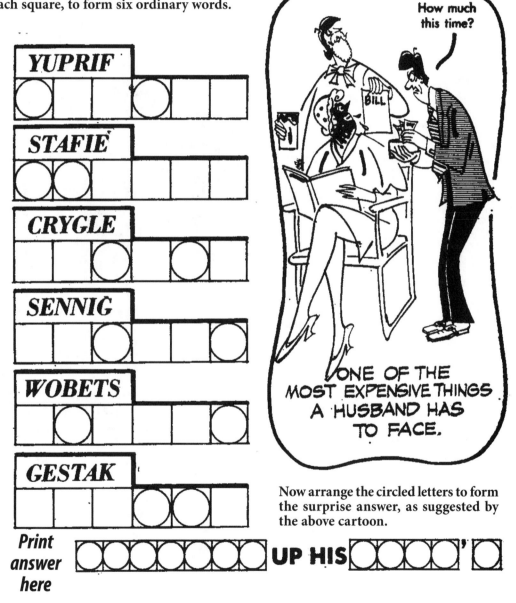

How much this time?

BILL

ONE OF THE MOST EXPENSIVE THINGS A HUSBAND HAS TO FACE.

Now arrange the circled letters to form the surprise answer, as suggested by the above cartoon.

Print answer here ⬚⬚⬚⬚⬚⬚⬚⬚⬚ **UP HIS** ⬚⬚⬚⬚⬚'⬚

171

JUMBLE®

Unscramble these six Jumbles, one letter to each square, to form six ordinary words.

KATINE

FLEMUF

CAJEKT

JENNIO

CURPSE

DALINS

WHY GIRLS
USE PERFUME.

Now arrange the circled letters to form the surprise answer, as suggested by the above cartoon.

Print answer here

TO ⬡⬡⬡⬡ ⬡⬡⬡ **BY THE** ⬡⬡⬡⬡

JUMBLE®

Unscramble these six Jumbles, one letter to each square, to form six ordinary words.

RIVACA

PANUCK

BALLEF

UMPAKE

SIXECE

ANQUIT

Giddyap!!!

WHAT YOU GET ON THIS FARM.

Now arrange the circled letters to form the surprise answer, as suggested by the above cartoon.

Print answer here ⬡⬡⬡⬡⬡⬡⬡⬡⬡ **&** ⬡⬡⬡⬡

173

JUMBLE®

Unscramble these six Jumbles, one letter to each square, to form six ordinary words.

DIZAWR

NORACE

MADENT

BETHIL

JELGUN

USUBED

Don't trust him

Don't trust him

WHAT THE CUNNING ACCORDIONIST PLAYED.

Now arrange the circled letters to form the surprise answer, as suggested by the above cartoon.

Print answer here ⬚⬚⬚⬚⬚ ⬚⬚⬚⬚ **AGAINST THE** ⬚⬚⬚⬚⬚⬚

JUMBLE®

Unscramble these six Jumbles, one letter to
each square, to form six ordinary words.

JERIGG

HERZIT

BRYDOW

GROHPE

RANTIM

GANFIC

WHAT A RAINY
DAY IS FOR A
CAB DRIVER.

Now arrange the circled letters to form
the surprise answer, as suggested by
the above cartoon.

Print answer here

JUMBLE®

Unscramble these six Jumbles, one letter to
each square, to form six ordinary words.

CASMIO

VONCLE

AGGIZZ

LUGGEJ

NAUCIV

VAQUER

Are they
wearing
anything
at all?

WHY MODERN SWIMSUITS
ARE REAL "COOL."

Now arrange the circled letters to form
the surprise answer, as suggested by
the above cartoon.

Print answer
here   **THEY'RE**   ◯◯◯◯◯ " ◯◯◯◯◯ "

JUMBLE®

Unscramble these six Jumbles, one letter to each square, to form six ordinary words.

GININN

FEINED

CAUABS

DURECE

SQUOME

WHYROT

THIS MUSIC CAN GET YOU A GIRL.

Now arrange the circled letters to form the surprise answer, as suggested by the above cartoon.

Print **THE** ⬭⬭⬭⬭⬭⬭⬭ ⬭⬭⬭⬭⬭
answer
here

JUMBLE®

Unscramble these six Jumbles, one letter to
each square, to form six ordinary words.

FLIDED

DINTUC

HAIDAL

LOWELY

RITHEE

FRIEVY

No problem now

HOW TO STOP
THAT NOISE
IN YOUR CAR.

Now arrange the circled letters to form
the surprise answer, as suggested by
the above cartoon.

*Print
answer
here* ⃝⃝⃝ **YOUR** ⃝⃝⃝⃝ ⃝⃝⃝⃝⃝

PUZZLE 176

JUMBLE®

Unscramble these six Jumbles, one letter to
each square, to form six ordinary words.

TELRUT

NOCHOP

RENUNG

TEASET

WINDAR

DIASUN

WHAT HAPPENED WHEN
THE GRAPES WERE
TRAMPLED ON.

Now arrange the circled letters to form
the surprise answer, as suggested by
the above cartoon.

Print answer here **THEY** ⬚⬚⬚ ⬚⬚⬚ ⬚ "⬚⬚⬚⬚"

179

JUMBLE®

Unscramble these six Jumbles, one letter to
each square, to form six ordinary words.

ENCLIP

TALCOE

DEBLOH

CLUDGE

BUCTAD

MEUMIN

WHAT THE SAILOR IN
THE TOP BUNK WAS.

Now arrange the circled letters to form
the surprise answer, as suggested by
the above cartoon.

Print answer here

JUMBLE®

Unscramble these six Jumbles, one letter to
each square, to form six ordinary words.

YASILE

TELEEB

MURBEN

HUTORF

SENCHO

ORPAND

You're late
for church
already

He'll hear
from my
lawyer

WHEN THE TAILOR WAS
DELAYED, THE GROOM
SUED HIM FOR THIS.

Now arrange the circled letters to form
the surprise answer, as suggested by
the above cartoon.

**Print
answer
here**
☐☐☐☐☐☐☐ **OF** ☐☐☐☐☐☐☐

JUMBLE®

Unscramble these six Jumbles, one letter to
each square, to form six ordinary words.

GALENT

BOTERD

LIKALA

HUNCAL

PHISOL

TUFACE

WHAT TO WEAR WHEN
YOU'RE GOING TO JUMP
OUT OF THE WINDOW.

Now arrange the circled letters to form
the surprise answer, as suggested by
the above cartoon.

**Print answer
here** **A**

JUMBLE®

Unscramble these six Jumbles, one letter to each square, to form six ordinary words.

JUINER

THARGE

KEPCAT

BAAMEO

INTIEF

GAVESA

WHAT THE SPANISH
FISHERMAN TURNED
DANCER PLAYED.

Now arrange the circled letters to form the surprise answer, as suggested by the above cartoon.

Print answer here **THE** " ⬡⬡⬡⬡⬡ - ⬡ - ⬡⬡⬡ "

183

ANSWERS

1. **Jumbles:** SNARL GUMBO FROLIC BISECT
   Answer: What the neurosurgeon's idea was—A BRAINSTORM

2. **Jumbles:** MURKY WHINE LACKEY FLOWED
   Answer: What the snake in the grass did when he was caught in the act—WORMED HIS WAY OUT

3. **Jumbles:** ETUDE SURLY BECALM FORAGE
   Answer: How the portrait painter expressed himself—HE MADE FACES

4. **Jumbles:** OWING DIRTY JURIST STOOGE
   Answer: How the pretzel maker got his alibi—TWISTED

5. **Jumbles:** DALLY ARBOR JUMPER SICKEN
   Answer: When it comes to words this guy doesn't have much of a flow—A DRIP

6. **Jumbles:** HIKER SNOWY FUMBLE DEFACE
   Answer: How the precise tailor spoke—IN MEASURED TONES

7. **Jumbles:** DECRY JUMBO INFUSE TAUGHT
   Answer: This could be the difference between male and female—AN ARGUMENT

8. **Jumbles:** TRULY WHISK SONATA VELVET
   Answer: What gold diggers go for in order to get diamonds—HEARTS

9. **Jumbles:** HOVEL PLAIT CREATE SOLACE
   Answer: This can be irritating as well as foolish—RASH

10. **Jumbles:** CHIME HOARY SKEWER AGHAST
    Answer: Some GI's consider this the sloppiest part of the Army—THE MESS

11. **Jumbles:** MOCHA PLUME JANGLE FIASCO
    Answer: Why they called the dizzy blonde "Bubble Head"—SHE WAS ALWAYS SHAMPOOING

12. **Jumbles:** AUGUR CHIDE BUTLER LUNACY
    Answer: This might mean nothing's been taken in—HUNGER

13. **Jumbles:** VIRUS POUND ADDUCE BEHELD
    Answer: The kind of creatures you might see in low-down dives—DEEP-SEA

14. **Jumbles:** HITCH STAID DULCET JITNEY
    Answer: This gets longer every time you cut it—A DITCH

15. **Jumbles:** CROWN INKED KIDNAP BENIGN
    Answer: What you might expect donkey's milk to have—A KICK IN IT

16. **Jumbles:** TWILL BOOTY KNIGHT JETSAM
    Answer: What the frustrated artist drew—A BLANK

17. **Jumbles:** GIVEN SHOWY WEDGED BEATEN
    Answer: This often covers a lot!—WEEDS

18. **Jumbles:** LOWLY PURGE THROAT BABIED
    Answer: A good bet for first graders—THE ALPHABET

19. **Jumbles:** WINCE DRAFT ACHING SUBTLY
    Answer: Why the snake lost the argument—HE DIDN'T HAVE A LEG TO STAND ON

20. **Jumbles:** CREEL IRATE BELLOW VENDOR
    Answer: This guy might tell you a story with a slant to it—ONE WHO'S NOT ON THE LEVEL

21. **Jumbles:** SLANT HASTY BREACH MARMOT
    Answer: Why the unsuccessful tennis player was offered a cigarette lighter—HE LOST ALL HIS MATCHES

22. **Jumbles:** CHUTE FAUNA SUBMIT TURGID
    Answer: Where a pedestrian might feel on edge—AT THE CURB

23. **Jumbles:** LITHE PILOT STANZA GARISH
    Answer: What you might find in that ol' swimmin' hole—"STRIP-LINGS"

24. **Jumbles:** VILLA NERVY BOUNTY SWERVE
    Answer: A kind of employee that might be found in TAVERNS—SERVANT

25. **Jumbles:** ALIAS TROTH BUCKET COMEDY
    Answers: What a boy who hates books might prefer to do—BAIT HOOKS

26. **Jumbles:** TARDY SHEEP AMAZON PURITY
    Answer: What the butcher turned actor got—MEATY PARTS

27. **Jumbles:** LILAC SPITE MEADOW ABSORB
    Answer: What the horse who flirted with the mare in the stable got—THE SAME OLD STALL

28. **Jumbles:** UTTER GROUP ENTICE NESTLE
    Answer: Why they couldn't find the fencing master—HE WAS "OUT TO LUNGE"

29. **Jumbles:** PRIOR TWINE DUPLEX RANDOM
    Answer: What a man who couldn't hold his liquor did—DROPPED IT

30. **Jumbles:** ANISE DRAWL CLIENT INCOME
    Answer: What skywriters write— AIRLINES

31. **Jumbles:** CABLE UNIFY GOSPEL HICCUP
    Answer: What the exterminator made the ants do—SAY UNCLE

32. **Jumbles:** ARMOR BULLY DEFAME HARBOR
    Answer: The alcoholic actor's favorite sandwich—HAM ON RYE

33. **Jumbles:** FOCUS POACH HECTIC INFANT
    Answer: How the correspondence romance ended—IN A PHOTO FINISH

34. **Jumbles:** BROIL NOVEL PALACE RABBIT
    Answer: What the baby who first saw the light of day on a plane was— "AIR-BORN"

35. **Jumbles:** CROAK PANSY BUNION GENTLE
    Answer: What the nude show turned out to be—A PUT-ON

36. **Jumbles:** FUSSY ROBOT DEVOUR ENTIRE
    Answer: What you might say when you see an intoxicated customs inspector—"SOUSE OF THE BORDER"

37. **Jumbles:** LOOSE CAMEL FALTER EXCITE
    Answer: What a fat man in a telephone booth might suggest—A CLOSE CALL

38. **Jumbles:** MINOR HOUSE SLOGAN LARIAT
    Answer: When lovers often have their big moments—IN THE SMALL HOURS

39. **Jumbles:** FIERY PAGAN MOBILE IMPAIR
    Answer: Where you might get mail in Ohio—FROM LIMA

40. **Jumbles:** ALIVE SKUNK DEMURE OPPOSE
    Answer: What a little soft soap can make—A MAN SLIP

41. **Jumbles:** CAMEO TEMPO CABANA POETIC
    Answer: What some politicians seem to want to tax most—OUR PATIENCE

42. **Jumbles:** BERET OPERA ANEMIA PONCHO
    Answer: The cheapest way to get to Europe—BE BORN THERE

43. **Jumbles:** LUCID HAVOC ARCTIC CANOPY
    Answer: This might be a break if you're a working person, but you can't bank on it!—A HOLIDAY

44. **Jumbles:** VALOR FUDGE CARBON MEMOIR
Answer: When it's wet, get under it! —COVER

45. **Jumbles:** SQUAW MINUS ESTATE DAMAGE
Answer: What the bewigged actor performed under—AN ASSUMED MANE

46. **Jumbles:** CURIO STOKE HOTBED DETAIN
Answer: The debtor's motto—"DUE UNTO OTHERS"

47. **Jumbles:** WOMEN BOUND WISDOM GADFLY
Answer: Lying like this can be easy—DOWN

48. **Jumbles:** COCOA ANNOY PILFER ELICIT
Answer: In the long run, this will benefit a writer!—A PLAY

49. **Jumbles:** DOILY WEDGE BOLERO STRONG
Answer: What little lambs often pull—THE WOOL OVER YOUR EYES

50. **Jumbles:** GLOAT HAIRY TURNIP SEETHE
Answer: To get a heavy date wear this—SOMETHING LIGHT

51. **Jumbles:** WRATH VOUCH SIMILE MISHAP
Answer: The only thing some women ever do on time—PURCHASE

52. **Jumbles:** TOXIN QUEER UPWARD JINGLE
Answer: The more lasting finish for a car than lacquer—LIQUOR

53. **Jumbles:** SYLPH REARM BURLAP ENMITY
Answer: The difference between a good speech and a bad one—A NAP

54. **Jumbles:** NEWSY GUARD EXHORT PATTER
Answer: What a lot of marriage ties are severed by—A SHARP TONGUE

55. **Jumbles:** TRACT SHEAF EXTENT LIBIDO
Answer: What the lawyer said as he ate an oyster—HMMM-HARD CASE!

56. **Jumbles:** BELIE YIELD INBORN GAITER
Answer: This might be the latest thing in weddings!—THE BRIDE

57. **Jumbles:** BERYL FORGO WATERY TYPHUS
Answer: Gives a beating that lasts a lifetime—YOUR HEART

58. **Jumbles:** TANGY FISHY BEWAIL WALLOP
Answer: What you wouldn't say to your old friend the antique dealer—"WHAT'S NEW?"

59. **Jumbles:** KHAKI SYNOD FETISH QUARRY
Answer: What a man who drinks like a fish rarely drinks—WHAT A FISH DRINKS

60. **Jumbles:** FOUNT VOCAL GYPSUM NOODLE
Answer: What they danced during the prison break—THE "CON-GO"

61. **Jumbles:** TAWNY VIXEN MARLIN EIGHTY
Answer: Growing old isn't so bad if you consider this—THE ALTERNATIVE

62. **Jumbles:** AMITY CRESS PRIMED SUNDAE
Answer: What both landlords and tenants often try to do—RAISE THE RENT

63. **Jumbles:** BEFIT FAKIR UNLOAD MUCOUS
Answer: What happened to the girl with the hourglass figure?—TIME RAN OUT

64. **Jumbles:** ZOMBI JERKY BYGONE DINGHY
Answer: What those who drink to forget always seem to remember—TO DRINK

65. **Jumbles:** ASSAY MOTHY ZEALOT TYPING
Answer: What a baby might be in warm weather—A HOTSY TOTSY

66. **Jumbles:** MOGUL GOUTY WEEVIL CASKET
Answer: What some weekend guests wear—OUT THEIR WELCOME

67. **Jumbles:** PUDGY SKULK UPROAR ELEVEN
Answer: What a man whose hand is quicker than the eye might get—SLAPPED

68. **Jumbles:** KAPOK QUIRE ASTRAY SAILOR
Answer: What you can expect a dozen rosebuds to come to—ROSES

69. **Jumbles:** SHEER AWASH DOUBLE FRIGID
Answer: What one deer said about another—I WISH I HAD HIS DOE!

70. **Jumbles:** BULGY JUICE AERATE CODGER
Answer: What a bright gold digger's weapon might be—HER "EYE-CUE"

71. **Jumbles:** FOLIO BEFOG INSIST POWDER
Answer: The easiest way to make ends meet—GET OFF YOUR OWN

72. **Jumbles:** KNOUT SUMAC HANSOM BAUBLE
Answer: A light kind of book—A MATCHBOOK

73. **Jumbles:** GAILY BALMY AFFRAY ENGULF
Answer: What getting up in the morning can be—ALARMING!

74. **Jumbles:** MANGY FUGUE PONDER LIMBER
Answer: What many who fly for a living wear—PLUMAGE

75. **Jumbles:** LYING BANAL MURMUR SALOON
Answer: When this happens, you might expect a pre-arranged uprising to take place—THE ALARM RINGS

76. **Jumbles:** ABOUT CEASE WHOLLY LANCER
Answer: What there was at the end of the burlesque act—A CLOTHES CALL

77. **Jumbles:** FEINT ENEMY RATION VACUUM
Answer: When you want to sleep this way, better put your watch under your pillow—"OVER TIME"

78. **Jumbles:** DECAY MINCE BARIUM HOURLY
Answer: How he paid his assistant—WITH MAD MONEY

79. **Jumbles:** LEAKY EATEN TAMPER PEPTIC
Answer: Up to the neck in hot water but continues to sing—A TEA KETTLE

80. **Jumbles:** HEDGE SCOUR MALTED UNLESS
Answer: What politicians who promise pie in the sky often do—USE YOUR DOUGH

81. **Jumbles:** HAZEL BATON DROPSY ARCADE
Answer: Make this and you're on the way up!—AN ASCENT

82. **Jumbles:** SANDY AWARD BLOUSE GOLFER
Answer: How she sounded when she tried to sing high C—"LOW-SY"

83. **Jumbles:** RABBI ELEGY BAKING FORBID
Answer: This is the best thing out!—A FIRE

84. **Jumbles:** WEIGH TASTY BEHIND UNLOCK
Answer: Why most things don't have to be thought out in modern kitchens—THEY'RE THAWED OUT

85. **Jumbles:** STUNG AGONY HINDER LEEWAY
Answer: What to say when asked to name the capital of all the states—"WASHINGTON"

86. **Jumbles:** CAKED SORRY FORCED MENACE
Answer: Because of this some movie stars are "cool"—FANS

87. **Jumbles:** ABOVE KNOWN CATNIP URCHIN
Answer: What a girl who says she'll go through anything for a man might have in mind—HIS BANK ACCOUNT

185

88. **Jumbles:** MILKY ESSAY PARLOR FOMENT
Answer: What people who don't summer in the country often do in the city—SIMMER

89. **Jumbles:** MADLY OXIDE TURKEY BOILED
Answer: A ten-letter word that starts with G-A-S—AUTOMOBILE

90. **Jumbles:** NIECE POWER CANNED MISLAY
Answer: You can make this but you'll never live to see it!—NOISE

91. **Jumbles:** ROBIN FLUTE EMPIRE FOSSIL
Answer: Where you have mountain ranges you might also find this—FOREST FIRES

92. **Jumbles:** BLAZE HUMAN WHEEZE POSTAL
Answer: What the inattentive student said when the teacher asked him to name two pronouns—"WHO, ME?"

93. **Jumbles:** PAPER TOKEN FONDLY INVEST
Answer: What the gossip was—THE "KNIFE" OF THE PARTY

94. **Jumbles:** ADAGE BRIBE PELVIS MYOPIC
Answer: Men look harder at girls who look this way—"EASIER"

95. **Jumbles:** FOYER KNAVE GALAXY BEMOAN
Answer: What a taxpayer hopes for—A BREAK IN THE LEVY

96. **Jumbles:** TARRY POKER DEBATE GYRATE
Answer: Often charged for better service—A BATTERY

97. **Jumbles:** POISE RIGOR HAMMER TONGUE
Answer: What the boxing champ turned circus performer became—RINGMASTER

98. **Jumbles:** LIBEL MADAM PYTHON FEUDAL
Answer: Serves to hold important things up—A DELAY

99. **Jumbles:** PRONE EXACT THIRTY GALLEY
Answer: Animals you might find on the golf course—LYNX

100. **Jumbles:** CYNIC GLORY IODINE AMBUSH
Answer: How a guy who starts the day with an "eye-opener" might end up—"BLIND"

101. **Jumbles:** FEVER MILK ENDURE BEACON
Answer: When a person's this, you wouldn't expect him to be a vegetarian—BEEFY

102. **Jumbles:** DEPOT RHYME RADIUS PURIFY
Answer: These people often change color—DYERS

103. **Jumbles:** NUTTY LUNGE ANSWER FUSION
Answer: Might help overcome difficulties with bottlenecks—A FUNNEL

104. **Jumbles:** ABOVE TWEAK CREATE POETRY
Answer: Island surroundings—WATER

105. **Jumbles:** HYENA AROMA JOBBER THROAT
Answer: What she called her boyfriend—"HER-MAN"

106. **Jumbles:** GOOSE TAFFY HUNGRY MUFFLE
Answer: Held up—at a public meeting!—THE FLAG

107. **Jumbles:** GUIDE CLOTH RECTOR DISMAL
Answer: What they were after being licked—MOIST

108. **Jumbles:** ALIVE WHOSE DROPSY TALKER
Answer: You can't do it in the middle—TAKE SIDES

109. **Jumbles:** PHOTO WEIGH BURLAP UNPACK
Answer: You wouldn't want to hurt this little dog but sounds like it—A "WHIP-PET"

110. **Jumbles:** WHILE NAÏVE FORCED INVITE
Answer: Could be wise—to fly at night—AN OWL

111. **Jumbles:** LINER AGILE BEATEN MUSTER
Answer: Sometimes shivers at mealtime—GELATIN

112. **Jumbles:** CAPON VALET MANIAC FERVID
Answer: People in complete agreement may speak with one—VOICE

113. **Jumbles:** REBEL UPPER PAROLE FLURRY
Answer: Made to measure—A RULER

114. **Jumbles:** LYING FEINT HIDING CUDGEL
Answer: How he conducted—LIKE LIGHTNING

115. **Jumbles:** CURVE PATIO QUARRY KOSHER
Answer: Used for an opening—A KEY

116. **Jumbles:** AMITY HEFTY PLAGUE INSIST
Answer: Food that makes apes tight—SPAGHETTI

117. **Jumbles:** ORBIT MOTIF BUMPER CANYON
Answer: Could be two cats making sounds like a drum—"TOM-TOM"

118. **Jumbles:** SWASH BLIMP JUNGLE PURPLE
Answer: What shooting anywhere might be—AIMLESS

119. **Jumbles:** LINGO DRYLY WISDOM VISION
Answer: No good will come to anyone from this kind of draft—AN ILL WIND

120. **Jumbles:** FORUM CAKED PREFER BRONCO
Answer: This blow was got from a scuffle—A "CUFF"

121. **Jumbles:** CHALK EIGHT VELVET UNTRUE
Answer: One—that might be worth more than any of the others—THE ACE

122. **Jumbles:** WAKEN ANISE BUCKET MORGUE
Answer: A Finn helped him to become famous—MARK TWAIN

123. **Jumbles:** AWASH FLORA ANYHOW KENNEL
Answer: What the absent-minded astronomer had—A FARAWAY LOOK

124. **Jumbles:** OCTET DOUGH ARTFUL EXPEND
Answer: An underwater traveler on a deadly mission—A TORPEDO

125. **Jumbles:** DICED GOING CANNED FATHOM
Answer: Sound as a bell!—DINGDONG

126. **Jumbles:** SAUTE DIRTY PEPSIN USEFUL
Answer: Damsels appealed to knights of old in this—DISTRESS

127. **Jumbles:** DITTY ABBEY LOTION CAUGHT
Answer: What to do after the overture—BEGIN

128. **Jumbles:** EJECT SHAKY MALLET WATERY
Answer: This direction might cause agitation—"SHAKE WELL"

129. **Jumbles:** ADAGE NEWSY COMMON MISUSE
Answer: Where to get married in Scandinavia—"S-WED-EN"

130. **Jumbles:** LYRIC POUCH NIMBLE CORRAL
Answer: This jail doesn't sound so hot—THE COOLER

131. **Jumbles:** KNELL PAGAN CARNAL VERSUS
Answer: What the nape might become—A "PANE" IN THE NECK

132. **Jumbles:** DOUSE EMPTY THRESH HYMNAL
Answer: How to get rid of tears—SHED THEM

133. **Jumbles:** LEAFY SYNOD DAMAGE STURDY
Answer: When tenderly affected by his horse—SADDLESORE

134. **Jumbles:** KNOWN TAWNY LOCALE GRASSY
Answer: How she found a shoe to fit—AT LONG LAST

135. **Jumbles:** APART DUCHY GYPSUM FILLET
Answer: He said this was the acting game!—CHARADES

136. **Jumbles:** GROIN HABIT PARODY IMPUGN
Answer: What the kangaroo's mate was!—HOPPING MAD

137. **Jumbles:** ABIDY RIVET FLORID OPIATE
Answer: Why the blond seemed more reasonable—SHE WAS FAIRER

138. **Jumbles:** DAISY PURGE PUNDIT UNFAIR
Answer: On this you should get to the top—THE UP AND UP

139. **Jumbles:** DOUBT OPERA SYLVAN AROUSE
Answer: Support an old-fashioned resting place—BEDPOSTS

140. **Jumbles:** LATCH GIVEN DEVICE IGUANA
Answer: Never try to do this with a witch—"HAG-GLE"

141. **Jumbles:** DERBY BANAL DITHER QUAVER
Answer: What was the outcome of all that activity at the brewery? —BEER

142. **Jumbles:** WEARY CROUP DENTAL LIZARD
Answer: This liquid can cause plans to change—COLD WATER

143. **Jumbles:** TARDY NERVY SOCIAL AMOUNT
Answer: What the end of the dynasty was—NASTY

144. **Jumbles:** AWOKE TUNED WAITER FORAGE
Answer: Noah put this together—TWO AND TWO

145. **Jumbles:** LUSTY HANDY LACING PENMAN
Answer: What working in the nursery was for the gardener—"CHILD'S PLAY"

146. **Jumbles:** AFIRE FLAKE TOWARD BENUMB
Answer: This kind of craft helps one to save—A LIFEBOAT

147. **Jumbles:** LIMIT GUMMY BEDBUG PIRATE
Answer: What one mountain climber wore—A "GETUP"

148. **Jumbles:** VIXEN FAVOR BANNER TURNIP
Answer: Big money—for a song!—"FOR-TUNE"

149. **Jumbles:** DINER GUESS VICUNA CUDDLE
Answer: Circumstances in which you might find yourself after going to one of those expensive health spas—"REDUCED"

150. **Jumbles:** ERASE IRONY PALLACE VELLUM
Answer: They often go out to sea at ports—PIERS

151. **Jumbles:** MAUVE TWEET BARREL HAZING
Answer: It doesn't pay him to play!—AN AMATEUR

152. **Jumbles:** OUNCE BRAVO RAREFY POCKET
Answer: Stock type—A BROKER

153. **Jumbles:** FLOOD GLAND MAGNUM REFUGE
Answer: In your throat, but don't worry—you won't croak! —A FROG

154. **Jumbles:** NOVEL GNOME ROBBER LAWFUL
Answer: What shorts may not be—WORN FOR LONG

155. **Jumbles:** FORCE ITCHY FEEBLE CANOPY
Answer: He sang as he played—OFF PITCH

156. **Jumbles:** DRAWL ODIUM HAPPEN ENTIRE
Answer: What it was for the auto thief—THE "END OF THE ROAD"

157. **Jumbles:** HELLO TRAIT GOITER DETAIN
Answer: If you're on it you'll be on time—THE DOT

158. **Jumbles:** LIVEN FOIST INVADE GUITAR
Answer: Taken unawares—STOLEN

159. **Jumbles:** VALUE IRATE PALATE EFFIGY
Answer: Has a rousing effect on servicemen—REVEILLE

160. **Jumbles:** BLESS DOWDY JERSEY ABOUND
Answer: The last thing the bride promised to do—OBEY

161. **Jumbles:** TRICKY BABOON VOLUME PODIUM TYRANT AVOWAL
Answer: What the reformed bachelor said his life now was—AN OPEN BOOK

162. **Jumbles:** GEYSER QUENCH CALLOW STUCCO HALVED BUTTON
Answer: What happened when Goliath tried some pot—HE GOT STONED

163. **Jumbles:** ORCHID HANDLE PASTRY NEARBY BEWARE CAUGHT
Answer: What some people go to great lengths to do—CHANGE THEIR WIDTHS

164. **Jumbles:** PIRATE COOKIE SENILE BANDIT RITUAL GENDER
Answer: These are often sensational at a beauty contest—TAPE RECORDINGS

165. **Jumbles:** YEARLY DIGEST OMELET MAGNET WAITER APPEAR
Answer: What 1969 pennies are worth this year—ALMOST TWENTY DOLLARS

166. **Jumbles:** BEHALF FERVOR MAGPIE HERALD UNEASY PURPLE
Answer: Why the run-down timepiece was rushed to the watch hospital—ITS HOURS WERE NUMBERED

167. **Jumbles:** TREMOR RATHER DEFILE INVERT GAMBLE FALLEN
Answer: How the bright rookie was signed up—RIGHT OFF THE BAT

168. **Jumbles:** PURIFY FIESTA CLERGY ENSIGN BESTOW GASKET
Answer: One of the most expensive things a husband has to face—KEEPING UP HIS WIFE'S

169. **Jumbles:** INTAKE MUFFLE JACKET ENJOIN SPRUCE ISLAND
Answer: Why girls use perfume—TO LEAD MEN BY THE NOSE

170. **Jumbles:** CAVIAR UNPACK BEFALL MAKEUP EXCISE QUAINT
Answer: What you get on this farm—QUACKERS AND MILK

171. **Jumbles:** WIZARD CORNEA TANDEM BLITHE JUNGLE SUBDUE
Answer: What the cunning accordionist played—BOTH ENDS AGAINST THE MIDDLE

172. **Jumbles:** JIGGER ZITHER BYWORD GOPHER MARTIN FACING
Answer: What a rainy day is for a cab driver—FARE WEATHER

173. **Jumbles:** MOSAIC CLOVEN ZIGZAG JUGGLE VICUNA QUAVER
Answer: Why modern swimsuits are real "cool" —THEY'RE REAL "GONE"

174. **Jumbles:** INNING DEFINE ABACUS REDUCE MOSQUE WORTHY
Answer: This music can get you a girl—THE WEDDING MARCH

175. **Jumbles:** FIDDLE INDUCT DAHLIA YELLOW EITHER VERIFY
Answer: How to stop that noise in your car—LET YOUR WIFE DRIVE

176. **Jumbles:** TURTLE PONCHO GUNNER ESTATE INWARD UNSAID
Answer: What happened when the grapes were trampled on—They LET OUT A "WINE"

177. **Jumbles:** PENCIL LOCATE BEHOLD CUDGEL ABDUCT IMMUNE
Answer: What the sailor in the top bunk was—UP ALL NIGHT

178. **Jumbles:** EASILY BEETLE NUMBER FOURTH CHOSEN PARDON
Answer: When the tailor was delayed, the groom sued him for this—PROMISE OF BREECHES

179. **Jumbles:** TANGLE DEBTOR ALKALI LAUNCH POLISH FAUCET
Answer: What to wear when you're going to jump out of the window—A LIGHT FALL COAT

180. **Jumbles:** INJURE GATHER PACKET AMOEBA FINITE SAVAGE
Answer: What the Spanish fisherman turned dancer played—THE "CAST-A-NET"

Need More Jumbles®?

Jumble® Books

More than 175 puzzles each!

Jammin' Jumble®
$9.95 • ISBN: 1-57243-844-4

Java Jumble®
$9.95 • ISBN: 978-1-60078-415-6

Jazzy Jumble®
$9.95 • ISBN: 978-1-57243-962-7

Jet Set Jumble®
$9.95 • ISBN: 978-1-60078-353-1

Joyful Jumble®
$9.95 • ISBN: 978-1-60078-079-0

Juke Joint Jumble®
$9.95 • ISBN: 978-1-60078-295-4

Jumble® at Work
$9.95 • ISBN: 1-57243-147-4

Jumble® Celebration
$9.95 • ISBN: 978-1-60078-134-6

Jumble® Circus
$9.95 • ISBN: 978-1-60078-739-3

Jumble® Exploer
$9.95 • ISBN: 978-1-60078-854-3

Jumble® Explosion
$9.95 • ISBN: 978-1-60078-078-3

Jumble® Fever
$9.95 • ISBN: 1-57243-593-3

Jumble® Fiesta
$9.95 • ISBN: 1-57243-626-3

Jumble® Fun
$9.95 • ISBN: 1-57243-379-5

Jumble® Galaxy
$9.95 • ISBN: 978-1-60078-583-2

Jumble® Genius
$9.95 • ISBN: 1-57243-896-7

Jumble® Getaway
$9.95 • ISBN: 978-1-60078-547-4

Jumble® Grab Bag
$9.95 • ISBN: 1-57243-273-X

Jumble® Jackpot
$9.95 • ISBN: 1-57243-897-5

Jumble® Jailbreak
$9.95 • ISBN: 978-1-62937-002-6

Jumble® Jambalaya
$9.95 • ISBN: 978-1-60078-294-7

Jumble® Jamboree
$9.95 • ISBN: 1-57243-696-4

Jumble® Jitterbug
$9.95 • ISBN: 978-1-60078-584-9

Jumble® Jubilee
$9.95 • ISBN: 1-57243-231-4

Jumble® Juggernaut
$9.95 • ISBN: 978-1-60078-026-4

Jumble® Junction
$9.95 • ISBN: 1-57243-380-9

Jumble® Jungle
$9.95 • ISBN: 978-1-57243-961-0

Jumble® Madness
$9.95 • ISBN: 1-892049-24-4

Jumble® Magic
$9.95 • ISBN: 978-1-60078-795-9

Jumble® Marathon
$9.95 • ISBN: 978-1-60078-944-1

Jumble® Safari
$9.95 • ISBN: 978-1-60078-675-4

Jumble® See & Search
$9.95 • ISBN: 1-57243-549-6

Jumble® See & Search 2
$9.95 • ISBN: 1-57243-734-0

Jumble® Sensation
$9.95 • ISBN: 978-1-60078-548-1

Jumble® Surprise
$9.95 • ISBN: 1-57243-320-5

Jumble® University
$9.95 • ISBN: 978-1-62937-001-9

Jumble® Vacation
$9.95 • ISBN: 978-1-60078-796-6

Jumble® Workout
$9.95 • ISBN: 978-1-60078-943-4

Jumpin' Jumble®
$9.95 • ISBN: 978-1-60078-027-1

Lunar Jumble®
$9.95 • ISBN: 978-1-60078-853-6

Outer Space Jumble®
$9.95 • ISBN: 978-1-60078-416-3

Rainy Day Jumble®
$9.95 • ISBN: 978-1-60078-352-4

Ready, Set, Jumble®
$9.95 • ISBN: 978-1-60078-133-0

Rock 'n' Roll Jumble®
$9.95 • ISBN: 978-1-60078-674-7

Royal Jumble®
$9.95 • ISBN: 978-1-60078-738-6

Sports Jumble®
$9.95 • ISBN: 1-57243-113-X

Summer Fun Jumble®
$9.95 • ISBN: 1-57243-114-8

Travel Jumble®
$9.95 • ISBN: 1-57243-198-9

TV Jumble®
$9.95 • ISBN: 1-57243-461-9

Oversize Jumble® Books

More than 500 puzzles each!

Generous Jumble®
$19.95 • ISBN: 1-57243-385-X

Giant Jumble®
$19.95 • ISBN: 1-57243-349-3

Gigantic Jumble®
$19.95 • ISBN: 1-57243-426-0

Jumbo Jumble®
$19.95 • ISBN: 1-57243-314-0

The Very Best of Jumble® BrainBusters
$19.95 • ISBN: 1-57243-845-2

Jumble® Crosswords™

More than 175 puzzles each!

More Jumble® Crosswords™
$9.95 • ISBN: 1-57243-386-8

Jumble® Crosswords™ Jackpot
$9.95 • ISBN: 1-57243-615-8

Jumble® Crosswords™ Jamboree
$9.95 • ISBN: 1-57243-787-1

Jumble® BrainBusters™

More than 175 puzzles each!

Jumble® BrainBusters™
$9.95 • ISBN: 1-892049-28-7

Jumble® BrainBusters™ II
$9.95 • ISBN: 1-57243-424-4

Jumble® BrainBusters™ III
$9.95 • ISBN: 1-57243-463-5

Jumble® BrainBusters™ IV
$9.95 • ISBN: 1-57243-489-9

Jumble® BrainBusters™ 5
$9.95 • ISBN: 1-57243-548-8

Jumble® BrainBusters™ Bonanza
$9.95 • ISBN: 1-57243-616-6

Boggle™ BrainBusters™
$9.95 • ISBN: 1-57243-592-5

Boggle™ BrainBusters™ 2
$9.95 • ISBN: 1-57243-788-X

Jumble® BrainBusters™ Junior
$9.95 • ISBN: 1-892049-29-5

Jumble® BrainBusters™ Junior II
$9.95 • ISBN: 1-57243-425-2

Fun in the Sun with Jumble® BrainBusters™
$9.95 • ISBN: 1-57243-733-2